SINGING IN THE
WILDERNESS

By Donald Culross Peattie

———————

Baltimore Oriole   ICTERUS BALTIMORE, Bonat.   Adult Male, 1. Male two years old, 2. Female, 3.   Tulip Tree, Liriodendron tulipifera

BALTIMORE ORIOLE

SINGING IN THE WILDERNESS

A Salute to

JOHN JAMES AUDUBON

By *Donald Culross Peattie*

New York
G · P · PUTNAM'S SONS
1935

Copyright, 1935, *by* Donald Culross Peattie

Fifth Impression, December, 1935

Printed in the United States of America
VAN REES PRESS · *New York*

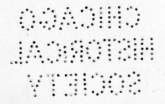

This book dedicated to Audubon himself may, the
author particularly hopes, please young Lisa who
also follows the birds....

NOTES ON THE ILLUSTRATIONS

BALTIMORE ORIOLE (Frontispiece). This is a characteristic example of the Audubon style, both as to color and with regard to drawing. It is plate xii of Vol. I of *The Birds of America* and was issued in December, 1827. It shows how Audubon broke with the traditions of museum or still-life bird painting, by representing the subjects in their living environment and in attitudes of animation. The adult male in flight at the top of the picture, and the very position of the leg of the female on the nest, were startlingly life-like for those times, and aroused the admiration of the public and many scientists, while it nettled cabinet naturalists and some rival illustrators. The nest of Spanish moss and the blossoming tulip tree were as unexpected to the eye accustomed only to European vegetation as was the black-and-orange plumage of this intensely American family of birds. Audubon records that he drew this picture in Louisiana, doubtless between 1821 and 1826. In the lot of the first dozen of plates to reach subscribers, it went far to make Audubon's reputation, along with the wild turkey which so pleased the sportsmen, the brilliant but faulty yellow-billed cuckoos, the grackles tearing open ears of corn, and the "Bird of Washington" (bald eagle) life-sized, which delighted American patriots. The *Baltimore Oriole* and the other Audubon plates in this book are reproduced, through the courtesy of the American Museum of Natural History, from a first edition (elephant folio) of *The Birds of America.*

MOCKING BIRD (facing page 8). The Audubon animation is here carried to an extreme. This formed plate xxi of the first volume, issued in December, 1827, and was seized on by Audubon's ill-wishers to raise the charge of Nature faking. The very fact that he had shown the most renowned of American song birds as the object of assault by the rattlesnake, the most deadly of our reptiles, was taken to prove the painter's sensationalism. There is little doubt that Audubon enjoyed this theatric juxtaposition. It was charged by naturalists that rattlesnakes do not and cannot climb trees and that no rattlesnake has recurved fangs such as are shown in the picture. Audubon's case was unfortunately compromised at this moment by an article in the *Franklin Journal* in which he gave a most accurate description of the black snake's method of constricting prey, but by a false trick of his memory, he ascribed the whole story to the rattler.

The controversy raged on both sides of the Atlantic, but finally specimens of a southern species of rattler were produced which have teeth exactly as Audubon represented them. It was also abundantly proved that the rattlesnake can climb trees. There is no record that Audubon actually witnessed the scene depicted, but on Aug. 25, 1821, at the plantation of James Pirrie at St. Francisville, Bayou Sara, Louisiana, he made an elaborate dissection of the dental arsenal and poison fangs of a rattler, representing the animal as "striking madly with its fangs." That study was doubtless the origin of the present plate. The heat on that day, he records, was so great that he could give only sixteen hours to the drawing.

Despite all criticism, this picture went far toward making Audubon's reputation with the European public. How it affected Lizars, the engraver, I have retold in my last chapter.

PASSENGER PIGEON (facing page 64). This

was plate lxxii in Volume I and represented a species of American game bird about which the sportsmen of Europe felt curiosity and envy. The immense quantities of these now-vanished birds, which Audubon reported as darkening the sky from horizon to horizon for hours, while the individuals were travelling sixty miles an hour, were doubted by many British naturalists. But the truth of the reports of their vast numbers is attested by all early accounts. It is remarkable that Audubon did not believe that this exquisite and valuable creature would ever become extinct, though he was probably right in supposing that the diminution in its numbers was due more to the destruction of the forests and their mast than to slaughter. There is no record of the time when Audubon painted this picture. He had probably made numerous sketches for it in his Kentucky sojourns, and when he came to make his final painting he was not necessarily on the scene; his sketches would have sufficed him to compose this peculiarly tender and animated study.

SELF PORTRAIT OF THE ARTIST, IN MINIATURE (facing page 116). This hitherto-unpublished likeness is here reproduced by the kindness of its owner, Miss Mary Stevenson of Chicago. The original measures two inches in length by an inch and a half in width, inside its solid gold frame. It was purchased in New Orleans, and according to a tradition that has descended with its owners it was made by Audubon for his wife, Lucy, probably on the occasion of a departure from her in Louisiana. The back of the locket, with a glass cover, was formerly filled with elaborately worked hair, doubtless Audubon's own. This was unfortunately destroyed while the miniature was being cleaned. It may be remarked that Audubon is known to have had the art of "working in hair," an accomplishment not then considered unmanly. The miniature is unsigned, but that is only natural if the locket had been intended for his wife. There can be almost as little doubt that this miniature is in Audubon's style of portraiture as that it is a striking likeness of the ornithologist, at about the age of thirty-six.

This portrait bears most resemblance to the Cruikshank miniature of 1831. The pose of the head is not quite the same in the two miniatures, and the present portrait represents a happier expression. The hair is light brown, the iris of the eyes is hazel, the pupils very large; the collar is white, the cloak russet and the tie blue.

The very existence of this miniature was apparently unknown to Dr. Francis H. Herrick when in 1917 he published his list of "Authentic Likenesses" of Audubon. He records that the ornithologist executed three other portraits of himself at about this time, one in oil in 1824, another in oil about 1826 and a pencil sketch in September, 1826. I have not seen even reproductions of these privately owned portraits, and cannot say what resemblance they bear to Miss Stevenson's miniature, which is however one of the four earliest likenesses in existence.

BARN SWALLOW (facing page 156). This rich and tender picture, plate clxxiii of Vol. II, was not the sort which, in Audubon's day, attracted great attention. Taste then ran upon life-size representations of game birds, or pictures informed with violent activity. A less sensational love of Nature has in our times brought a proper appreciation of this phase of Audubon's work. There is no record of the when and where of the original sketch for this plate. It was issued in 1831.

SNOWY HERON OR WHITE EGRET (facing page 216). Issued in 1834, this was plate cclii of Vol.

III, but the drawing was made in all likelihood in the neighborhood of Charleston, S. C., in October, 1831. The picture is notable for exhibiting Audubon's unique gift of magnifying the minutest details of plumage in the foreground, while keeping a distant background, with the most attentuated perspective, still clear and arresting. Note the characteristic plantation house in the distance, and the southern vegetation. In this case Audubon has dared to add a middle-ground that also disputes our attention, with the fowler spying on the bird.

The intense naturalism produced by many of the Audubon paintings is due to this *tour-de-force* of representing foreground, middleground, and background with equal clarity, just as they appear in life to our eyes, instead of merely sketching or indicating all but the central object of interest. Even the photographic lens seldom gives the illusion both of close-up and clearly defined distance, or if it does so, it must, as a rule, greatly exaggerate the attenuation of perspective. The Audubon style, whatever may be said against it artistically, is a marvelous approximation of the way in which the human eye records foreground and distance simultaneously. I would point out, too, that Audubon has not succumbed here to the temptation to make his bird graceful or to fit it into a composition. The snowy heron is already beautiful enough without prettifying it, and he has caught the true spirit of the heron family by representing this member as a stiff, startling creature who looks wholly real and at ease neither on land nor in the air.

FORK-TAILED PETREL (facing page 234). In August, 1831, while returning to America in the *Columbia*, Audubon had himself lowered, during a calm, in a small boat in mid-ocean to study the "Mother Carey's Chickens." These proved to be fulmars and several species of petrels, including the present.

Every observant ocean traveller has noticed that the gulls do not follow the ship more than a few hundred miles from land; it is only in mid-ocean that the strange, sooty little petrels, half gulls and half swallows as they seem, appear suddenly and mysteriously, winging round and round the ship. They are the very spirit of the wildest wastes of ocean, skimming down the long hollows between the waves, cleaving through the spray, never at rest as they flit, the color of storm-clouds, in the world of sea and air. Audubon has here captured their eery charm, and once again has broken with previous tradition, by representing one of the birds almost upside down, partly in order to show naturally the white markings on the underparts, partly to express the wave-tossed, wind-buffeted life of his fleeting subjects. This was plate cclx of Vol. III and was issued in 1834.

SINGING IN THE
WILDERNESS

I

THE SKY was the color of a junco's wing, but the juncos were leaving, this early spring day, and the flickers were moving in—they call them "high-holers" here in mid-continent. To reach the cabin on the edge of the woods I had to wade out in my boots through the high April sloughs. It stood on a rise of dry ground, under three giant bur oaks; and there was a pile of firewood under a tarpaulin, by the door. I got out the key and let myself into the one room. It was still and cool, and smelled of unpainted wood and old wood smoke. There on the wall were his paintings of the winter wren, the barn swallows and the fork-tailed petrels. There was the typewriter under its cloth, and there the clean quires of paper. Out of my tired arm I threw down the books I should need, and I knelt and touched a light to the firewood laid on the hearth.

Many appointments in this life advance as if predestined. One is obliged at least to be present at one's birth and death. And in this very wood, years ago, I had kept the third great tryst of a man's life. But there are other romances he may have, beside the love of woman. And now I was here, to come close together with a man to whom I had grown to feel myself uniquely bound.

The fire was getting lively, and I pulled a bench to the hearth, sat down and filled a pipe. I heard the log talk, and the lisp of my pipe, and the sweet bubble and trill of the swamp tree frogs. I was glad to be back. It was my first American spring after five years, and all my country was fresh washed for me as scenery after rain. I could smell the ozone of it. My angers with it dropped away.

There had been years I nourished them, for greater pleasure in my exile. The air I breathed then was drenched with the odor of orange blossoms, and the nightingale sang all day and all night. I had a villa with a dedicated cook and on my table the wines of the country; my wife had a soft-spoken Italian maid who loved to look after her frocks, and my children spoke perfect French and played in the sunlight every day of the winter that was not winter. I went swimming each summer morning in the Mediterranean with the punctuality of a man going to his office, and when I was sweetly exhausted I lay on the hot rocks near other people's handsome bodies and contrived new chapters for novels about worldly people.

And then one day I fell homesick. I was homesick for asters under the trees, for the thud of hickory nuts in the wide autumn air. Homesick for the crow's cry, and the hawk's shadow, and a flicker's wing on the sunburnt grass beneath the oaks. I wanted to hear the long, lonely sound of an American train whistle calling off the miles, five thousand of them from ocean to ocean, and all of it America. I remembered Willow Slough where the sandpipers mince, and the redwinged blackbird pool, and the cabin in the woods, and even the bird prints on the walls. But men or nations seldom choose to turn and take the way back to first simplicities. Then the exchange went against Americans, and so, for no very noble reason, I came back.

It was a strange thing, and one on which I hadn't counted, that even when I got here I was still homesick for America. I wanted something that did not come. Perhaps some of it went forever with the bison and the passenger pigeon and the tepee. Thinking as a naturalist, I can never forget that the people who call themselves Americans are an inquiline species, successful invaders, like dandelions or house sparrows. But it isn't all gone, the living America underneath the mechanical. My country, the part of it that God made, is something, I found, that I could never make any foreigner feel, even a little. You cannot tell him about the Wilderness Trail, or the Gettysburg Address, or the white-throat singing, or the Great Smokies. If you want to speak of these things to your heart's satisfaction, you have to wait for a man who loves them as you do.

I put a log on the fire, beginning to feel more sure that I was approaching John James Audubon. I sat poking at the log and wondering why I proposed to write about him. There were several biographies already in existence, and I had, actually, no time for this rendez-vous. The notion was out of step with the march of my life that had quickened to the American pace since my return. It was probably unprofitable, and I had a living to earn—something at which Audubon himself was never particularly successful. (That was one of the lesser bonds between us!)

I left the fire and stood with my hands in my

pockets, looking at the man's bird paintings on the wall. From the first edition, elephant folio. Why had I bought them, long ago, in a moment of extravagance that was somehow far-sighted?

I began to examine my absurd claim, that was really only a wish, to know private and particular things about a man whom others had studied so exhaustively. I could claim, of course, that the part of my country that he knew best was also my part. My childhood introduction to Nature had been in the South; that had been, again, the first field of my serious endeavors in my student days. The Middle West, the Old Northwest of Audubon's day, was my country too. And his France was my adopted country, my second love.

But these comparisons were merely notional. My need to talk about John James Audubon went deeper than any human desire to talk about oneself. Yet I could not claim that I had learned particulars concerning his life, heretofore unprinted. Nor did I wish to disturb the great Audubon legend; that he lived to protect bird life was a noble fiction. But I wanted to speak for the man himself; I wanted to tell of him as all Americans love to tell each other Lincoln stories. Our listeners have usually heard them before, but even so, we cannot hold them in; they let something escape from our hearts into the open; they let the winged best of us free.

So I found at last that the wellsprings of my great sympathy for Audubon were bubbling up from a love of what he stood for, as Frenchman, American, artist, loafer, wanderer, lover, bird-hearted observer. He was all these things in an age when the worthy pioneers, my ancestors, were slaying the passenger pigeon by the thousands every day and then driving in their hogs to fatten on the iridescent corpses. It was an era when men set fire to the towering hardwood forests, the last virgin wilderness of the temperate zone, because it did not vanish fast enough.

The fear of beauty, the contempt of self-distinction, these things he faced. Almost alone among immigrants he came neither to seek gold, nor stake land, nor escape a consequence at home. He had the genius—and the fatal defect—of all the French in the New World, lightness of hand. Spaniard and Englishman and all the rest, they came to this continent as conquerors. Its furnishings they thought fit only to be swept away and replaced by their own. The French alone loved America as she was. They passed through the land reverently, leaving no memorials to themselves, leaving no scars. They were the only Europeans who were ever successful, more than momentarily, at keeping peace, and their own honor, in their dealings with the Indians.

I was leaning against the window, looking at the old woods young with buds. This way such men as Joliet and Marquette and Tonty had journeyed, *en portage* between the Chicagou and the Des Plaines. They had not left a trace of their going, save a few trees, bicentenarian now, bent at the odd unmistakable angle that marked the portage trail. The sword of France had passed through this country and cut no more than the wind. The Fathers of France had braved Indian torture fires to make converts, but they hanged no witches, turned no thumb-screws. Now of France nothing was left here but a few soft names —Fond du Lac, Prairie du Chien, Vincennes, Charlevoix, Desplaines.

Against the English colonial policy, the empire builders of New France were sure to fail. They built an empire upon wind, where God was better served than State, and that is the country into which we did not grow. I heard the roar of the none too distant metalled highway, the pride of the county, the repeated battleground of police and killer. The roads of New France were the heron-haunted rivers and the silent, shining lakes.

New France was gone, politically, when Audubon came on the American scene. But he was of it, none the less. He was the last of the voyageurs, the last of the chevaliers, the last of the troubadours. And, of course, to the pork-hominy-and-hymns of the Old Northwest civilization, he was a Quixote de la Mancha. What he lived for was fantastic. And it was the best.

I think we shall have more need of him as time goes on. There are birds, a number of them, that we shall never see now except in his drawings; and more, he is our youth and we are leaving it every day. But Audubon goes deeper for me than this. It is the purity of his motives that shines out so grandly. They look as exceptional and worthy in my America as in his. They were no more nor less than curiosity and delight. And these are the essence of science and art.

Now the benefactions of the artist and the scientist are great and they are spiritual, but they are not direct. It is the precious task of other temperaments, the teacher, the saint, the inventor, the doctor, to apply pure spirit to earthly needs.

PLATE XXI

Mocking Bird. TURDUS POLYGLOTTUS

MOCKING BIRD

This temperament is richly bestowed upon America. We comprehend it and we give it room and help. It is more difficult for us to be patient with a man who does not seem to care how the world is going, who is so little occupied with humanity that he does not even put his own family first.

So men caught John James Audubon in the toils of bankruptcy; they saw him to jail; they laughed him in the face for a fool, and they sold the copper plates of *The Birds of America* for old junk.

Now, Audubon has been canonized as one of our national saints. In New Orleans, where he and his wife and children almost starved to death, there is a fine statue of him, with English sparrows hopping on its head. And fame came to him even in his day; newspapers carried items concerning every movement of the great man. Long after, men were proud to say that they could remember him.

But I wanted to talk about the Audubon of the wilderness years, I wanted to remember him as a child. Here historians have walked most warily because they have the fewest and the shakiest facts. But I felt confident about telling the things one cannot know save as the story-teller knows, by intuition, what must have happened to his characters, what words alone could have been spoken. Such facts as there were should serve me as blazed trees. The rest it would be my delight to search for, in a great love of Nature, of France, of our American past, of childhood and young romance.

First I would go back, a long way and a long, long while ago, to the little boy that Audubon had been, a waif of destiny, a child who loved birds with a curious passion. I would go back to the marshy fields that he knew then, beside the Loire. I would call up the kind, chiseled features of the people who nurtured that child. I would try to feel the soft gray-gold French sunlight of a vanished cycle, and listen for his friends the fieldfares and ousels and skylarks that died, unmarked on shore and hill, so long ago.

So the story began to come to me, like something seen through the wrong end of my binoculars, something very small and bright and far away. At first only the little figures moved there; then words, a few speeches, blew to me across the years, and even the bird notes from the trees reached me. And I began to write it down.

II

DOWN THE rue de Crébillon in the heart of the old city of Nantes, a carriage came clattering, to draw up before the façade of a certain tranquil house. Three street boys building dams in the gutter scrambled out of the way, and stood staring as the carriage door opened. Out stepped a stocky, hearty gentleman in the uniform of an officer of King Louis Sixteenth's navy. He turned and offered his arms to the dark interior of the carriage, and a moment later there stood on the pavement a boy of four in travel-stained finery, with a handsome, inquisitive face. The gutter-snipes stared, and he looked back at them out of his brown eyes with friendly curiosity. They knew in an instant that he was a stranger to their city, and he seemed to be examining them and their play as if they were small birds of a sort he had never seen before. All his life long he was to look thus at the world, friendly, curious, a stranger, and finding nothing commonplace.

But the street boys, looking beyond him, saw a sight to make their eyes bulge. Emerging from the carriage was an immense negress of a West Indian type, with high cheek bones and cannibalistic lips. As this ogress lumbered in her flouncing petticoats to earth, they saw that she carried a tiny girl in the crook of her coal-black arm, a travel-weary little thing who crouched against her shoulder, half hiding a face of the doll-like whiteness that comes to European children brought up in tropic countries. A white-headed old black had clambered down from his seat beside the driver and was shouldering a battered sea chest.

"*Alors, mon petit* Fougère," said the officer, and he took the little boy's hand in his big one, "the long voyage is over. This is your home."

Then the door to the house opened. The little maid who held it gave a cry of surprise and turned back into the house. The boys in the street heard her calling,

"Madame, Madame! It is the master, come home! The Master!"

As the captain and the little boy, the negress with the baby and the laden old black entered the open door, the children in the street could see the staircase within, and a short plump lady come hurrying down it in a rush of billowing silks. They saw her open arms, and how she knelt and gathered into them the strange little boy from far away, and then the house door closed upon the rue de Crébillon and the placid old city of Nantes.

The child Fougère marched up the treads of the stairs with his hand in the soft plump hand of the lady. Her mountainous skirts stormed and rustled beside him; lace fell from her white wrist over his hand enclosed in hers. Glancing up, he could see little of her, only her rich bosom with the glittering brooch upon it, and the folds of her white fichu. So close had he been clasped against that breast upon reception that he had not seen her face, but made acquaintance rather with her fragrance of lavender water and the warm softness of her neck where his little nose was buried.

She was clucking like a hen, as she led him up the stairs. "Up we come! Up we come! You still feel the deck under your feet, don't you, *mon enfant?*"

Now they were at the top of the stairs—two flights—and the child was led into a room full of airy northern sunlight, under steep pitched eaves.

He peeped back over his shoulder and saw Theresa
lumbering up the stairs, still bearing Muguet and
walking with that sullen sidewise gait, one hip
and shoulder hoisted. Used to watching her face
like a weatherglass, he read her suspicious resentment.

To the nurse Theresa this room was small and
ignominious. She wanted the great, dark, stately
nursery in her master's plantation house at Les
Cayes, back in Santo Domingo. There, behind
the shelter of the green shutters, closed against the
familiar swelter of heat, you could see yourself
and the dim cascade of the mosquito curtains
faintly reflected in the long solemn mirrors. There
she had ruled it over her charges, decreeing when
they should eat and sleep, when they should be
washed and dressed. Now already the white mistress was ordering her about in a running torrent
of purest French. Theresa pretended not to understand her, cradling the baby girl fiercely. The
little maid came in bringing towels and hot water
in a big basin. With positive plump hands
Madame Audubon took the child from her nurse.
Theresa muttered. Giving little outcries and ex-
clamations, Madame stripped off the spotted
finery that clothed the little girl. All the rents

that Theresa never darned because they did not show, were coming to light. Fougère recognized the tropical hurricane gathering on the nurse's black brow.

The little boy's eyes were misting with weariness. As in a vision he saw his little sister, undressed and meagre as a new-hatched birdling, standing in the great bowl, in the sunlight, and the lady kneeling by her and sponging her, mourning over her thinness. Then for himself came the healing of hot water, the comb through his hair, the great relief of stretching out in quiet sheets. And at last he was seeing the lady's face clearly, looking up into that flushed, benignant plumpness where the lips smiled and the eyes twinkled for him. She kissed him. At once his loyalty was bodily transferred from his nurse to this new tender presence. He said very seriously, *"Merci, Madame."*

"No, no, mon petit!" she said with too bright eyes. "Not 'Madame.' Call me *Maman.*" And he heard that she begged it of him.

She went out, calling on Theresa to follow her. But Theresa was lingering, looking around the walls for house snakes and tarantulas. As soon as Madame Audubon had left, she went to the

green shutters and closed them firmly. The muf-
fled bang expressed all her pent up contempt for
this room, for France, for the white mistress.
Then she tramped out.

The child Fougère lay in his bed for a few
minutes in the gloom that Theresa had cast upon
it, wondering if the time had come when he could
assert his manhood and defy his nurse. His
father, he knew, did anything he wanted with the
blacks. His father appeared to be the richest,
grandest and most powerful person in the world.
He had fought pirates off Cape Haitien and sunk
a British ship, and had been with Admiral de
Grasse at Yorktown when Cornwallis surrendered.
His mother, he knew, was in heaven with God
and the angels, and a great deal of the time his
father was away, beating the English. Until this
moment Theresa had loomed omnipotent in Fougère's life.

Now suddenly he slipped down out of the big
bed and in his nightshirt and bare feet went across
to the window and climbed up on a ladder-backed
chair to push open the green shutters defiantly.
The sweet, moist air of the northern spring blew
in upon his face and breast, and he saw that before him lay a world of roof tops, all the old blue

and gray steeply pitched gables, the intricate chimney pots and the soaring spires of Nantes. Across the way was a mossy gabled roof with a weathervane upon it. In the tiny square of garden below him a tree gushed up from the ground like a fountain and fell in a fine spray of limber yellow twigs faintly budded with the tender green of April.

Spring was a season that the child had never known; there were no springs in Santo Domingo, only the great dry season and the great wet season, and the little dry and the little wet. All you could say of spring in Les Cayes was that, from being hot, the plantation became a furnace, when even the blacks would not walk in the sun. Then the last of the winter birds flew off, to North America, his father had told him when he asked, and there were left only the gorgeous chatterers and trogons in the mango trees, and the little sugar birds who came tamely into the green gloom of the rooms and hopped about on the furniture, apologetically picking up insects.

Now this foreign spring filled his lungs with a temperate elation. Already the sea air had breathed a new energy into his little tropic-born body. Every sense in him was alert, and when

upon the weathervane across the way, a speckled and glossy black bird alighted, he spied it on the instant. First it preened a while, and turned its shiny neck this way and that, then it ducked its head and scraped its feet, and presently it made a sound like cracking nuts and spitting out the shells. Then it began to whistle as if insistently calling a dog. After this it talked; Fougère could not understand what it said, and it had not occurred to him until this moment that in all the world there were other birds than those of Les Cayes. Now he realized that this was a French bird, and whatever it said was bird French. And it was certainly speaking some sort of a language; it croaked and gabbled and clucked and whispered, and now and then its neck feathers would tremble while it made a whirring sound in its throat, as if it were a mechanical bird and its little spring inside had just snapped and run down. And then the wind changed, the weathervane veered sharply round, and the starling dropped out of the little boy's sight as if it had been shot.

His golden laughter broke about the room. But in her bed the child Muguet slept on, in the pool of her hair, her white wrists flung up on the pillow beside her.

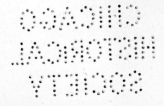

In the polished drawing-room downstairs, ("a flummery little show box," the officer thought fondly,) Captain Audubon and his wife Anne were met at last. Madame was seated erect upon a small chair, which she filled capaciously, with her plump hands lightly laid, one on the other, in her short lap. Madame remained quite calm. The Captain, on the contrary, paced up and down the room, waiting for his wife to speak. This was, the Captain told himself, a supreme test of their marriage. All the inequalities piled up between them would have to be reckoned with now. For, after all, he had married a woman nine years older than he, a woman with her own property, a woman who could and doubtless would judge him from her superior height of greater virtue and—here in Nantes—firmer security than his. On the deck of his ship, on the *galerie* of his plantation house, he was master of wealth, a man who both used and protected the bodies and lives of others beneath him. Despotism was demanded of him by the circumstances. Sailors as well as slaves would not have recognized any milder rule as rule.

He ran a finger around his neckcloth, and still she did not begin.

"You got my letter from New York, telling
you I was bringing them?" he demanded.

"But certainly," replied Madame Audubon.

"Good," said the Captain, again pacing the
Aubusson carpet as if it were deck planks. Aboard
ship that would have sufficed; with that you could
have dismissed the mate from the bridge.

But his mate remained quietly seated. She remarked, "The boy is very like you, Jean. Handsome and winning. Tell me about him."

He arrested his stride, brooding. Yes, tell her
about him, he thought, mocking himself. Tell
about old Dr. Sanson slashing his horse through
the green wall of the jungle rains. Putting his
periwigged head between the ghostly mosquito curtains that concealed the woman in the bed. Tell
about the birth of his only son, and the death of
the woman he had most loved, in the dim, swelter-
ing room, where the bats banged against the
ghostly green mirrors.

"His mother's dead," said the Captain
brusquely. It sounded as harsh, as dry as the report in the log of a burial at sea.

"Who was she?" asked Madame Audubon
quietly.

"Call her—call her Mademoiselle Rabin," he

said. And by that Anne Moynet Audubon knew that the mother's real name, or her full name, would never pass his lips; that she had been some one highborn and lost.

"And the girl? You wrote that she was not the boy's full sister."

"Half sister," said Audubon. "Her mother was Catherine Bouffard."

"She is dead too?"

"Can't say. It wasn't I who sent her away." And by that Anne Audubon knew that this other woman he had held more lightly, for that she had been lighter. She had vanished, perhaps without a thought for her babe.

The Captain flung his hands out to thrust through the silence of his wife. "You cannot understand, Annette. Here in Nantes—well, it's a world for women like you. It's Europe. Christian. Settled. Bells ringing all the time, bells for baptism and confirmation and confession and marriage and burial. Everything ship-shape and done according to the articles of navigation. God watching you."

He went over to the window and stood with his back to her, looking out into the rue de Crébillon, with its houses crowded one against the other, where every man was jealous of his neighbor's rectitude and saw that he kept to it. But the walls went thin before him and he saw Les Cayes—the pier shimmering in a haze of heat, the sound of the blacks' singing wafted over the tobacco and indigo fields, the tinkle of a lute from behind the closed green jalousies of the great central bedroom.

"Out there, in Santo Domingo . . ." he said, and fell silent. He began again. "It's another world. A black world, black and gold."

"I cannot imagine it," she said, and shook her lace-decked head.

"I might defend myself, I suppose," he told her, turning from the window, "by a reproach to you that you did not come out there with me. But I would not have had you in that climate or that society. They corrupt. And yet you, if you had come, would have remained unchanged. I'm not like you, Anne. Not many people are."

Now she knew that though another woman had carried his heart to her grave, his honor he had confided forever into her own hands. The unshakable security of her wifehood filled her with triumphant pride. Trusting him now once more, she at last trusted herself to speak, and her passion of

indignation gathered in her plump breast. Lifting
his humbled gaze, he saw the storm upon him, and
before he could reef sail it broke.

"But how are you to be forgiven? How could
you so neglect them? They both looked like little
rubbish bags, and thin, but so pitifully thin!
Where was your heart, that you could entrust them
to that terrible black cannibal? Heaven knows
what she has fed them! And the girl has been
carried all her life, apparently. She barely walks!
But then how could she, on those poor little legs?
And what clothes you had dressed them in! Frippery, Jean, frippery! Only a man would buy such
things for his children."

Never had the Captain looked for the high
winds from that quarter! He bent his head to them,
his heart glad within him, for they were blowing
him to harbor.

"And 'Fougère!' " she went on. "And 'Muguet!'
'Fern' and 'Lily-of-the-Valley!' Are those Christian names for good French children? Where on
earth did you get such a pagan fancy, Jean?
Surely with those names they can never yet have
been baptized. Why, they might have died, there
in Santo Domingo, and gone to God as little
heathens. I shall see the curé about it tomorrow."

An immense relief and gratitude humbled him. "Then you are willing to keep them, Annette?"

Suddenly she burst into tears, covering her face with her hands, her plump shoulders shaking with sobs. So many years had gone by for her here alone in Nantes, utterly alone, a barren woman to whom it was a blow upon the heart even to pass children in the street!

"When they have come at last!" she cried out, and put a hand forth blindly to him.

He took it, and bent to lay an arm in comfort about her. He did not understand the sources of this tempest of tears. But let it blow, he thought. He was in port, with two anchors down.

III

AUDUBON WROTE, in later life, of Anne Moynet, "Let no one speak of her as my stepmother. I was always to her as a son of her own flesh and blood, and she was ever to me as a true mother."

As to the woman who bore him, his feelings were deep and secret. He fabricated a tale for the world that his father had wedded a Spanish belle in New Orleans, "as beautiful as she was wealthy," but no one else seems to have heard of her. And all too many dreamy plantation houses under the live oaks of Louisiana boast themselves the birthplace of John James Audubon. But that he said once he loved Louisiana better than any other in the union, must content the Pelican State.

Until twelve years ago no one could say any more of the true birthplace and mother of Audubon than the little that he himself vouchsafed. He never said anything more definite than that he first saw the light in the New World, and that his own

mother's name he had never been permitted to
speak. He maintained that he did not know his own
age within four or five years.

Audubon had a mystery to conceal, and in spite
of the fact that no two of his tales concerning his
origin agree, he would have been quite successful
in veiling the truth, but for the national French
passion for preserving the most trivial records.
Rummaging among such waste paper, F. H. Herrick, Audubon's most thorough biographer, discovered a bill rendered a hundred and fifty years
ago to Captain Jean Audubon of Les Cayes by
that not at all fictional physician, Dr. Sanson.
There, among doses of ipecacuana, tincture of
rhubarb, *eau blanche*, Hoffman's mineral liqueur,
bleedings, and vaccinations, for blacks and master, appears the name of a Mademoiselle Rabin.
From the medications scrupulously noted and un-
scrupulously charged for, she seems to have been
in frail health. The night of April 24th, 1785, the
doctor passed at her bedside—item, 66 francs.
Night of April 25th, ditto. It is not until the 26th
that in a small hand Dr. Sanson dryly notes,
"Mademoiselle Rabin is delivered."

Of what young life, terse documents reveal by
intricate deduction. The archives of Nantes yield

the act of adoption of Fougère and Muguet by their father, Captain Audubon, but the lad Fougère is sixteen years old before the church records set forth his baptismal name, Jean Jacques Fougère Audubon. Step by step the gracile signatures of the young Frenchman alter; "Fougère," with all its painful associations, is dropped; the fanciful name "La Forest" is tried on and discarded, and at last the American hero writes his name, John James Audubon.

It is the old Captain's will that provides the link between him and the babe born in dark Haiti to an unknown woman. In that document he appears as Jean Rabin, and only thus. The chain is thus complete.

Audubon was in America when this will was made known to him; according to family tradition he refused his inheritance rather than admit to the name Rabin. But a letter has come to light that accepts both, only to waive his patrimony in favor of Rosa, his sister, the little Muguet of so long ago.

So much for the facts that underlie the tale, inscribed in spidery official hands on all that old rustling paper. The feelings that color it are vouched for by the portraits before me of Anne

Moynet Audubon and her husband. They face me from the page, well mated. The Captain shows the elements that are ascribed to the male, fire, command, the courage to lay hold on life; his lips are humorous and tasty; his eye is knowing and his nose self-willed. Opposite him, under a filmy and beribboned cap—a triumph of millinery—Anne looks complacently forth. If that is a prayer book she holds in her hand, it is there simply for adornment, like the jewels in the lobes of her ears. Her plump flesh speaks of good living, her mouth is indulgent, and she looks on life with a mixture of practicality and sentiment.

The blacks that Audubon says accompanied the Captain and his children to France soon vanish from the story. So too must the little boy's first memories of Santo Domingo have faded in the cool French air. All that in after life he could recall was that from the first his father had taught him to look at birds, and that before he knew that the tops of the trees did not brush the skies, birds were for him "a frenzy." Years later he wrote of himself as a child, "None but aërial companions suited my fancy."

They suit the fancy of us all. What they feel they can voice, as we try to. They court and nest, they battle with the elements, they are torn by two opposing impulses, a love of home and a passion for far places. Only with birds do we share so much emotion. Man feels himself an infinity above those creatures who stand, zoölogically, only one step below him, but every human being looks up to the birds. They seem to us like emissaries of another world which exists about us and above us, but into which, earth-bound, we cannot penetrate. It is not the strength of the lion that we give to angels, but wings.

And I think there is not any man to whom some bird call will not reach, to remind him of things he thought he had forgotten. The call of a crow makes me smell sunburnt grass, the chuckle of a wren has in it all the invitation of April, the running of Blue Ridge brooks, the honeyed odor of azalea, the light feet and heart of holiday. Any day that I hear the kingfisher's rattle it will be moonlight for me when I was lost once and lay blanketless upon the ground to sleep, and heard that war cry above the rushing of a nameless stream.

And there are joys and hours of trouble that, remembered long after, bring back the birds which flitted so unconsciously across them—there were two petrels, once, between the slippery hollows and the hissing hills of the sea, a thousand miles from land; if they could ride out their storms, I thought, then so might we.

Another man may remember a farm childhood in the west, and the Franklin's gulls, strange inland dwellers, that follow the spring ploughing like white crows. The chatter of sparrows reëchoing in the cold stone court of a hospital. The kittiwakes that followed after him when he had left every other friend behind on the vanished shore.

Each year the robin's first uplifted optimism, served up as blithely as if it were new, will make your law-abiding, care-worn citizen believe again what he thought when he built his house and planted his flowers and his children.

If you and I are so stirred by the swallow's spiral and what the heron calls back over his green shoulder, then what that child new come to France so long ago felt in his heart for the birds who spoke to him, was a passion.

To reach the house, La Gerbetière, where Captain Audubon retired with his family in the summer, the carriage rolled out of cobbled Nantes, where jackdaws in the old coigns cocked a thievish eye after it. Then it bowled along through the flat

useful lands, starting up the carrion crows in a
cloud of black petulance from the furrows. And at
last it rolled through gray Couëron, and the boy
in his chosen place on the seat beside the driver
would turn his face up to the wheedling and dis-
puting of the swallows as they eddied about the
heavy stone Breton spire. An old owl lived in there
who said "Boo! boo!" to frighten village children.

When it was sunset time, and an air heavy with
salt from the estuary rolled up the meadows, the
carriage would drive up to La Gerbetière's gates.
The family unpacked into the house. Then his stepmother would find all the things that the maids
had not got ready. His father would throw open
drawers, looking for lost papers and wanted tobacco. Rosa would find the doll she had left here,
smelling of damp and shut-away, and sit on the
floor to comfort it. But Jean Jacques would run
away, with the after-glow full in his face, to the
tidal meadows where the fishing dories lay stranded
on mud and flaccid eel-grass, and the redshanks
and curlews minced on their long, mis-jointed legs
and found out about things with their bills.

He woke in the mornings to the talk of pigeons
on the roof, rolling their delightful French *r's*
deep in their gentle throats. There was a whole

tower for them on the barn, and they used it like a barracks from which a dozen times an hour they swept out upon the field of air, wheeled around as one company, swooped so low that the chaff and the weeds trembled from their wings, rose like a river in the sky, and breaking their descent with a stiff and silky rustle, alighted at their cotes, nodding their heads to one another and a-roo-coo-cooing.

From his father's prize orange trees came the whistle of a blackbird, which is like the song of a thrush who has somehow been made perfectly content about life. The old cook had tried to teach him to throw stones at blackbirds to chase them from the fruit, but he only threw his stones to knock down apples.

When the chaffinch called it was time to get up, and thereafter all day was playtime, until at last he was old enough to pass under the shadow of lessons. Then he learned the art of tiptoeing past his father's door after breakfast, where awaited him the dreaded mathematics without which he could never rise to be even a gunner, much less a captain who knew every rock between La Rochelle and the great Gray Nose of Calais. If he succeeded in escaping, he evaded too the English language, harsher than the talk of starlings. When he came back with a cuckoo's egg in his pocket and a bag of sweets charged on a limitless account in the village, with mud on the limp white ruffle of his shirt, the Captain would be waiting for him, patting his right knuckles in his left palm behind his coat tails.

But Anne Moynet Audubon rustled between them, offering the fond untruth that she had sent the boy expressly to the village to tell the tinsmith that the spouts were clogged with leaves.

"Well, sir," the Captain scoffed, "did the tin-smith throw you into the Loire? You look like a little mudlark."

"Jean!" reproached his wife, flinging her arms about the boy as if protecting her fledgling from a hawk. And then, lifting the child's chin on a dot-ing finger, "You are the handsomest boy in France, and if your father were not an old sea tartar, he would not keep you forever at those lessons."

On such a day a young peasant came into the court with a half dozen of thrushes hung by their throats on an iron hook that swung in his hand. Germaine the cook came to the door, and a grimace of refusal wrinkled her time-pitted Breton face; she had ordered a joint for today. It was the child

Rosa who called her brother to come and see. She
was staring in horror and pity at the dead song
birds with their little wry necks, hating the young
hunter's red hand that ruffled back the breast
plumage. Jean Jacques came idling over the old
stone flags of the kitchen, munching a cake, curious and amicable. When he saw the strung up
thrushes, he swallowed the last of the cake with
a gulp, and light flared up in the brown eyes. The
man was turning away, when the little boy pushed
past the cook and called out with a lordly fa-
miliarity,

"*Eh, toi! Attends un peu!* Wait, what are you
going to do with those thrushes?"

The peasant stopped and laughed over his
shoulder. "Put them in the pot," he said.

Jean Jacques took the little kill of birds in his
hand and lifted the weight of them from off the
hook. "There is not enough on their bones to feed
a cat. It's stupid to kill them to eat. I'll buy them
all."

"What can you want with them?" said the
young man in his thick tongue.

The child had taken one into his hand, and his
head was bent over it absorbedly. "To look at."

He paid out some coppers as if they had been

louis, and gave one of the birds to Rosa, who went off with its limp body pressed to her cheek, and held a funeral over it under the currant bushes. Jean Jacques passed through the kitchen with his purchase in his cupped hands.

"What are you going to do with those?" demanded Germaine, the old family tyrant.

"Keep them," said Jean Jacques.

"You won't keep them long," predicted the cook. "Whew!" She never let you do anything without spoiling it just a little bit.

Jean Jacques walked through the cool of the salon, gazing down at the spotted breasts, the dainty bills, the little stiff claws clutched only on death. His sentiment was not pity nor horror, but something keener and happier. He was sorry the birds were dead, but it was heaven to hold them in his hand. He had ambitious projects for stuffing them, but he knew he did not know how to do this, and that Germaine was right; he had no way to keep them. But his father would know something to do, and he went and knocked on the study door.

The Captain was unexpectedly sympathetic. To give himself time to think, he took a snuff box out of his waistcoat pocket, took a pinch, closed the box and tapped it.

"I have to keep one, at least," Jean Jacques was explaining gravely. "I can never get close enough to them in the trees. And if I bury mine like Rosa's I'll not have it to look at any more."

His father peered with fellow feeling at the limp thrushes. He turned and pulled a book from his shelves, and ruffled its pages. "Well, here you are," he said, pointing to an illustration. "You can always come and look at this."

"But it won't be the bird as I saw it," said the boy obstinately, and then he had the inspiration that was the beginning of *The Birds of America.* "I'll draw my own picture of it! I've got the crayons you gave me on my birthday."

"My pencil gave birth to a family of cripples," Audubon admits in his memoirs, but every year it was his custom to throw away everything he had drawn in the past twelvemonth, and start all over. So it is that there are extant no Audubon drawings before those dated 1805, the nineteenth year of his life.

Audubon credits his father with a critical encouragement of his drawings. "He was so kind to me that to have listened lightly to his words would have been highly ungrateful. I listened less to others, and more to him, and his words became my law."

But he obeyed a law higher than his father's. Only an artist would feel the compulsion of that cruel and courageous decree that doomed to yearly destruction the drawings he had so loved and labored over. It was a habit which he retained his life long, and it is one more index of the strength and prodigality of his powers.

So his golden childhood passed away, and manhood of the Napoleonic era faced him at sixteen. His parents had striven to give him an education extraordinarily liberal; there was place in it for music and dancing, fencing and drawing, English and geography. Judged by the standards of that age, his was a thoroughly spoiled childhood. But its chief result was a thoroughly sunny and tender character.

The Captain and his soft-hearted wife gave to their boy every instruction that should enrich his life as a gentleman. But it was not as a gentleman that he passed it. It was Nature herself, claiming him for her own, who best armed him for the path ahead, that led into the wilderness. And the child hiding in the harsh salt grass to watch the gathering of the green sandpipers was pre-

paring himself for those ice-locked weeks beside
the Mississippi when his merchandise lay spoiling
on the shore and business ruin stared him in the
face. Then and there in Missouri's woods he took
his profit, in terms of teal and mallard, whistling
swans and wild turkey. The ledger that Audubon
kept balanced values that other men could not see.
To be free, to be true, to follow a bird in the woods
or an impulse with his pencil, these were riches
when all else was destitution.

IV

THE *DOSSIER* of Captain Audubon, preserved in the office of the Marine, shows that, having a knowledge of the English tongue, in 1799 he was in Albion, arranging for the exchange of French prisoners. On the night that he got back to his wife Anne and his children, he asked his daughter to show him her *cahier*. Rosa brought him the lesson book timidly, and the Captain, looking very judicial, glanced over the pages and from time to time remarked "Hm." He handed it back with a smile. Her heart glowed when her father smiled; it was like seeing spring come to a tough, thorny tree. His approbation was worth working for.

"Those are very good, my dear," he said. "I don't see how at fourteen we could have much more in our curly head. And what progress have you been making with the virginal?"

Rosa smoothed the back of her frock in a fluff toward her knees and took her seat at the instrument. The wiry notes chimed about the drawing-room in a minuet. Captain Audubon put his finger tips together and closed his eyes attentively. Jean Jacques looked at the candle light through the glass prisms of the chandelier, because the gentle, twinkling lustre was like the pattering notes of the virginal. Madame regarded her two men folk and happily swung her slipper toe in time to the minuet, her capped head nodding the beat.

Concerning her little stepdaughter she was fully satisfied, and so she gave her little thought. But the two Jeans had entered her life too disturbingly ever to be merely family; they were romance to her, intimate strangers in whom she had a singing pride. They were like as two coins, she thought, struck only in different years—the same warm flashing eyes, the same fine head, one in a white peruke, the other with shining light brown locks to the shoulders. The same quick flare of temper, and the same rainbow smile after the storm. With her each could do what he liked, but in one another each had met his match. The minuet pirouetted to an end, and the Captain clapped his long hands. There was a little rustle of success about Rosa.

"Well, now, Jean Jacques," said the Captain, "what have you to show us?"

"Come and see," said Jean Jacques, rising. And he held open the door for his father.

Rosa and her stepmother accompanied him pridefully upstairs, after Jean Jacques. The boy opened the door of his bedroom upon some very dubious odors and a chamber cluttered like a museum. A parrot rasped in its cage, "*Rien pour pauvre Mignonne?*" And a small marmoset ceased from turning over three kestrel's eggs in a box and leaped guiltily to the top of the mirror.

"Here, see this, *mon père*," said Jean Jacques. "I finished stuffing it only today. A corn-crake."

The Captain picked it up in appraising fingers, on its little stand of dried peat. Sod and bird, the specimen seemed to weigh no heavier than a copper. It was, the Captain admitted inwardly, a practically perfect taxidermic job.

"*Bon Dieu!*" cried Madame Audubon suddenly. "Is that a viper, my child?"

"Oh, yes," said the boy nonchalantly. "I bought it from one of the boys at the Green Farm. He had killed it only that day. A pity he couldn't have done it more neatly."

"Very thoughtless, truly!" chuckled the Captain.

Rosa observed, with a small fastidious nose uplifted, "It smells, in here."

"Well, now," began the Captain, clearing his throat.

"I want you to see this clutch of plover eggs, Father," his son said hastily. "Do you know how I blow them out?"

And before his father could answer he had thrown open a drawer and pulled out a series of drawings. He began to prop them up against the wall and on the floor, chattering.

"This whinchat is no good, but the green woodpecker isn't too bad, is it? And this hoopoe. I traded a shoe buckle for its body."

Rosa gasped, but her brother rippled on like a brook. "Nightingales are hard to do just because they're so easy. I mean, they're such plain little birds. Oh, and here's a dabchick. I winged that myself. I'm really an awfully good shot now, Father. I can put a bullet right through a tossed up cork, at twenty-five paces."

When there were no more pictures, he went to the wall and snatched down the fencing foils and flexed one judicially in his long fingers.

"I'm quicker on my feet than I was. Do you want to take me on for a bout and see? If the ladies won't scream too much!"

"Perhaps," said the Captain, thumbing his chin. "I shall have to see your lesson books first."

"Now my dear Jean," broke in Madam Audubon placatingly, "remember that the boy has just got over the measles."

"Let us see the books he did before he had his measles," suggested his father liberally.

Madame made a hopeless little gesture with her plump hands, and Rosa looked cheerfully at her fingernails. With one glance at the Captain's face, his wife brusquely put the girl out and followed her.

Audubon reports that at the state of his formal studies, he could only hang his head. His father looked at him with speculative eyes and walked very lightly out of the room, humming a little tune.

Next morning two wagtails were picking up a breakfast of beetles on the terrace, with jerky little clockwork runs, when the house door opened. The Captain and Jean Jacques emerged, followed by a servant bearing the boy's trunk and violin case. The wagtails bobbed away down the garden path in surprise. The autumn morning sparkled with dew, and the shadows of the trees in the orangery were long and velvety. From the wall a redbreast lisped his sweet autumnal song. But he could not hold back Jean Jacques. The future had rushed upon the boy, to carry him off.

At the gate the carriage waited, and the family gathered. Rosa brought from the garden a sweet william for her father's buttonhole. Madame bent and gave her son an enfolding embrace; under cover of it she slipped a shower of coins into his pocket. With the gaiety of one who will soon return, the Captain kissed his wife and daughter and stepped into the carriage. The boy was folded once again in his mother's arms; he and Rosa kissed each other on the cheek, and then he leaped up to his place, and the impatient horses started.

From the window he had a last glimpse of his mother's face, crumpled with anxiety, her fingers at her lips. Rosa waved a blithe goodbye. The whip cracked and the horses began to trot, whirling him away. La Gerbetière was gone. Within a few minutes gone too would be Couëron, gone at last the generous Loire, and all his aërial companions, that alone suited his fancy.

The pulses in the boy's throat beat excitedly.

Almost any adventure might lie ahead of him. He might be going to Paris to see the crowds and the buildings and bridges and parades of the capital. Perhaps he was going to sea. After all, his father had run a cruise at thirteen, as a cabin boy, and been captured at Louisburg and languished five years in a prison hulk in English waters, where he had imbibed the English tongue and a hatred of Albion not quenched even at Yorktown. If indeed, Jean Jacques felt, he must leave his beloved, treasure-laden room at La Gerbetière, leave Brittany and the Loire, then he would let the longing to travel possess him utterly.

But his father had made their destination mysterious. In his corner the Captain took out of his pocket a volume of Montaigne's *Essays* and began to read. There was something about that gesture that suggested to the boy that his father was already half removed from him. Jean Jacques had a premonition that never again would his mother's indulgent wing be spread over him, and that the gulf beyond the nest yawned below him. Between his father and himself there was still love—the boy never doubted that—but he did not suppose it to be infinitely indulgent. He looked to his father to be right and brave and wise; he depended upon him for the utmost justice. But what he dreaded now was that his father was going to mete out some of that justice.

With this dismal prospect ahead, Jean Jacques turned to the carriage window and looked out, seeking to forget the ominous present in the aching beauty of Nature. He did this instinctively without thinking, and with a crying heart he saw how free seemed all the world except himself. The swallows were gathering into little wheedling, departing bands for their flight to the south. Cows were stepping, leisurely, into a slow stream, and a girl, who had never, probably, had a lesson in her life nor would have, hurried her geese out of the horses' way. How gladly would he have let her stand in his shoes, at that moment, could he but take her barefoot place in the dust amidst the nasal fowl! Everything but himself was free, free as the breeze that stamped now right, now left, upon the rippling grain and on the darkening river.

While Jean Jacques yearned out of the window, his father took occasion to steal a glance at his child. Montaigne had been nothing but a blind; behind the *Essays* the father hid from the possibility of questions. If it had been any other boy in the world, he could have brushed all questioning aside, but any father who implies that his motives need not be made known to his son is running away from the penetrating gaze of his own lost innocence. As he looked at the boy's features, less awakened to life than even Rosa's, and remembered the time-pocked leer of some face thrusting up through a hatch—he could not recall where he had seen it, perhaps on every voyage—he felt like the wicked father of *Petit Poucet*. He cleared his throat with a sound like Jove's thunder, and returned to Montaigne, whose dry words jigged in time to the wheels and the stones.

In this fashion—so Audubon recorded years after—did he and his father travel for several days, only necessary remarks passing between them, until they rolled inside the walls of Rochefort and drew up at the door of a house that his father possessed in that seaport town, France's naval stronghold.

The Captain whipped out his key and tramped into the hall, where the coachman set down the trunk. Jean Jacques with his violin case followed his father wonderingly into the salon, where the Captain was throwing open the shutters to let in light upon a room in which a woman's hand had had no making. There was an elaborate model of a ten-gun sloop upon the mantel, flanked by the two sea-green bottles with tiny brigs inside them, and on the walls were yellowed coast charts with marks and fathoms in microscopic figures all over them. On a very long table stood a ship's clock which his father immediately set by comparison with his watch. Then in a gesture he commanded his son to sit down.

"*Mon enfant*, we can talk here as man to man. No frills and petticoats. You must have felt hobbled. But you're all right now. The whole French navy's in port, and we're safe."

He took a turn about the room, and the boy smiled into his neckcloth.

The Captain wheeled back. "I've neglected you. If I hadn't come back they'd have had you doing embroidery. Now you're going to work. You've got to work." He paused. But his son made no protest; he had known that so much at least was coming. So the Captain went on, "I'm going to superintend your education. I don't mean I'm going to teach you. There are men better fitted than I am for that. You are going to the best school in France, to my way of thinking."

He saw the boy's face chill, though he kept his chin up, and he went on more kindly. "I don't mean there won't be any leisure, or pleasures to fill it, but the remainder of your time *must* be employed with industry and care. As for today, it is ours together. I've affairs to see to, but if you want to see the docks, the ships-of-war, and walk around the wall, come along."

It was already a deeply ingrained trait of Jean Jacques' character to meet destiny with the courtesy of a good grace. He rose, smiling, as though all that his father ordained was a pleasure to him. And in truth that day he tasted one of the sweetest and most stirring joys that may come to a boy—the sight of his father standing high among men of his kind.

The Charente and the ship basin were thick with masts as the banks of the Loire with trees. There was a stiff breeze snapping at the many flags, and sunshine dancing on the water. As they went stepping over coils of rope and out of the way of trundled barrels, the Captain would halt every now and then, with his hand on his boy's shoulder, to present him to some officer magnificent in sash and sword and cocked hat.

"Another Audubon, eh, to bring the British colors down?"

And Jean Jacques would put his best strength

in the clasp of some big hand, and square his shoulders.

By the time the guns in the fort had fired the sun down, Jean Jacques Fougère Audubon was enrolled in the military school, and a young officer was inspecting his uniform with an eye that tarnished every button. With the back of his hand he shoved in young Audubon's stomach and with the other thwacked him between the shoulder blades to push his chest out.

"Put your head up! Pull your chin in! Lock your knees!" he roared.

Jean Jacques, the perfection of military obedience, fired a broadside of rebellion from his brown eyes. Gabriel Loyen du Puigaudeau grinned at him with friendly insolence. A good lad, this—fire in him. He would have chuckled if he had known that the handsome boy had a sister even prettier whose arms would one day be about him. And Jean Jacques would have relaxed in relief from that agonizing attention if he had guessed that the officer before him was merely his future brother-in-law.

For some months the boy endured the glamorless grind of the fortress and the training ship, the parade ground and the vermin-ridden old bar-

racks. Each day the clock crept round as slow as
the sun through the twelve signs of the zodiac.
Only at evening was he freed, with his fellow cadets
who poured out upon the town, pushing each other
to be first to get at the precocious pleasures that
made the boy's lip curl back in disgust yet set his
heart to pounding in his ribs.

New Year's Day passed, with presents from his
mother—a ring and a jingling purse and a box
of sweets. From his father there was a book on
the life and campaigns of Turenne, with an in-
scription about the duty of a French boy to his
country that sounded exactly like one of the Com-
mandant's set speeches. Wanting them too much,
and ashamed of it, Jean Jacques thrust his mother's presents in the bottom of his kit, and tried to
forget them.

For three weeks more the gruelling continued.
Then one tingling morning in January, his old
enemy, mathematics, betrayed him. A mounting
column of unmanageable figures rose up at him,
mocked him, menaced him, toppled over him, till
he sprang from his desk and ran like a wild thing,
skimming like a lapwing, close to the ground,
through the gardens of the Secretariat of the
Marine.

But the bird was caged. His flight got no farther than to the bars. A deserter, he was marched back, and within the hour he was sitting in the darkness and stench of the prison ship, cringing away from the ex-galley slaves, the incorrigibles and sweepings of the jails emptied by revolution and war. The food he ate, the water he drank, the talk he heard, the things he saw done in that hold of punishment, he was never to forget, nor the moment when he was called above decks to face his father, who had returned to buy his release at the price of begging from men who could have been proud to sail under him.

When he got back to his old barracks, Jean Jacques, aching for comfort, dived into his kit. But the louis and the ring were gone; the box of sweets was empty. With thoughtful delicacy, the jackdaws had left for him the *Life of Turenne*.

V

TIME SOFTENED Audubon's recollections of his boyhood trials, leaving but a few salient moments of anguish, which, like the rest of us, he was perhaps inclined to over-emphasize. But probably nothing could exaggerate his experience of the prison ship. And though the details he gave are scant enough, I found it easy to feel what he did not tell. I remembered my talks with a sensitive nineteen-year-old French boy called up for training with the Chasseurs Alpins, and all that he had told me of the theft and the lice, the uproar and the constraint of the barracks. I remembered the sight of those barracks, of the sentinels at the gates, of an officer with his little *baton* stooping down to peer along a whole company of legs, sarcasm in his eyes. I remembered the dirty *bistros* that clustered just outside the gates, and the girls who walked by in the evening.

A full half of every man's life is made up of motions and encounters that are eternal, that do not vary greatly from one epoch to another. There, with Audubon's memoirs to guide me, I felt safe enough in my rôle of dramatist. Sometimes Audubon tossed me a detail, one out of a thousand he must have forgotten, like the hummed tune with which his father turned his back on those neglected lessons. (Had he not remembered that little touch, I would have been proud, as a writer, to have invented anything so lifelike.) But Audubon's memory was as fallible as his mathematics. It was so far flawed that he could report the death of two brothers in the Revolution, when they must have been uncles if they existed at all. And his biographers, whenever they have gone behind his *ipse dixit*, have had to rewrite his life for him.

So when I encountered what he recalled that his father said to him in the house at Rochefort some thirty years before, I looked again at the Captain's jocular and forthright countenance, and I ventured to doubt some of those polished syllables and change them without changing their meaning. Any one who has read Audubon's writings extensively will realize that he makes Daniel Boone and the Baron Rothschild, President Jackson and Charles Lucien Bonaparte and the Captain his father all speak in the same idiom. In short, it is Audubon's idiom, and perhaps not even precisely that, for the English of his writings was, at least in some cases, carefully polished by others in the polite style of the early nineteenth century.

Audubon's memory, or rather, his forgettory, has flung a charitable cloud across the rest of his year at school. The family was in Nantes when Jean Jacques in his cadet's uniform stepped smartly from the Rochefort coach and swaggered through the streets, with the guttersnipes eyeing him in awe. Rosa was deeply impressed, and all through the first meal sat watching her suddenly glorified and romantic brother. There was a pheasant for dinner, and the boy's favorite dessert of wild strawberries and cream cheese. There was the old soft warmth to cradle him, the old adoration of him, but now he felt how undeserving he was of it, knowing himself better, and received it the more gently.

With the Captain's return from business, the family moved out again to Couëron, to La Gerbetière, and there were the wagtails, rocking themselves across the terrace; there were the cool sweet rooms, smelling a little of damp and shut-away. Madame went about, finding dust on the prisms of the chandeliers where the soft June sunlight

broke in a shower of colored notes. Rosa discovered that last summer's frocks were now too short for her. The Captain found mould in his snuff tin, and Jean Jacques opened the door to his old room that he had left for Rochefort when he was only a lad a year ago.

Mignonne's perch was empty; carpet beetles had ruined his stuffed owl. Mice had knocked his box of eggs to the floor and broken them. But the little corn-crake still stood upon its stand, subtle of plumage, elegant of stance, and carefully tied in their portfolio his drawings lay waiting for him where his mother had left them.

He tugged the green bow eagerly open and threw back the cover to the first drawing. In some cold light of manhood he saw the redstart as a child's pathetic effort. He threw it aside and turned to the green woodpecker. Wretched. A stick; out of drawing! He tore it up in pitiless fingers. The willow warbler fared no better. That study of the head and bill of a jackdaw wasn't too bad, but what was a fragment? In a few moments nothing was left but a heap of torn papers on the rug.

In his study, the Captain crossed a final seven, put down the Santo Domingo accounts, and reached for those of "Mill Grove," the estate in

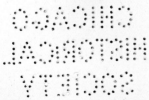

Pennsylvania. This Miers Fisher was an honest man and a cautious agent, but he was slow and thick of wit, the Captain thought. What was needed was a quicker eye on things; a pity the Atlantic was so wide. There was a knock on the door.

Jean Jacques came in, and closed the door behind him. Well, they had squared his shoulders for him there at Rochefort, at least, was the Captain's fleeting thought, and there was pleasure in the eyes that rested on his son.

"I want to speak to you, *mon père*, seriously," said Jean Jacques. "About my future."

"It is my constant thought," said the Captain dryly. "I am glad you too are beginning to think seriously about it. Sit down."

But the boy roamed the room restlessly. "I've got to learn to draw," he said to the carpet.

"Why?" inquired the Captain.

"To do my birds right. They're so stiff. You couldn't imagine them flying."

The Captain regarded his son, and saw that however trivial this sounded, it was a matter of immense importance to the boy. So he said nothing and waited.

"It's a question of technique, I suppose," said

Jean Jacques, with far speculation in his eyes. "Well, I could learn that."

"And the navy?" suggested the Captain briefly.

"Oh, I'll never be any good at that!"

"How hard have you tried?"

"You are thinking of the time that I disgraced you and myself. Well, suppose, if you had been longing for the sea, when you were sixteen, they had shut you up in a theological seminary to become a priest. Wouldn't you have jumped out of the window and got away to the docks if you could?"

Despite himself the Captain smiled. "Are you suggesting that you would like to become a priest?"

"*Parbleu, non!* I don't know what I will become. Not a soldier. Not a sailor." He could not, or would not, go on, but in his head were the birds, and the knowledge that they alone concerned him.

The Captain sat back and rubbed his chin speculatively. A son all his own he would have known how to raise. But Jean Jacques was but half his. He moved the bronze Cupid on his desk, and asked,

"An artist?"

"Not like other artists," said Jean Jacques help-
lessly. "But I want to learn to draw."

Out of doors, a chaffinch piped suddenly from
the orangery, as though reminding the Captain of
something.

After all, the boy was *hers,* too. He had never
wholly understood her; he had only given her what
she wanted. Her room and her flowers and her lute
he had never quite regarded as his, although in
his house; they were part of herself, things be-
fitting her. If she had asked something else, anything except his career of the sea, she would have
had it. Was she not asking him only that her child
be given his own career? The boy seemed to have
some notion of his own destiny, was indeed helpless before it.

"Just what do you expect to do with your life,
my boy? I might add that I cannot open for you
any or all doors, or even so many as I might have
earlier. The times are hard."

Jean Jacques was never as concerned about the
family fortunes as he knew he was expected to be.
Money, it seemed to him, should come from God,
like fresh air. But with caution and tact he argued
to his father that what he wanted would cost less
than the training at Rochefort. Fluently he dis-

coursed upon the advantages of a broadened education, the opportunities of the capital, all unknowing that his father had already yielded to him. When he had reprimanded the boy on the deck of the prison ship at Rochefort, under the eyes of officers, he had said the stern things which were expected of him. But he knew then that he had done the boy wrong in trying to cut him after his own pattern, and that the next time Jean Jacques asked anything of him he would have to grant it.

So now he slapped the desk with his hand and said, as though he were yielding at last in despair, "*Eh, bien,* you must go your own way, then. I'll let you go to Paris. Put you to school under David. He's the best there is. He was here in Nantes and painted the mayor's portrait."

Jean Jacques began to thank him, and was cut short.

"I cannot imagine what your mother will say to this notion," declared the Captain, with a gesture that flung all hope to the winds. "The school at Rochefort was a nunnery in comparison with Paris. You will have to look out for yourself there. I shan't be able to get you out of scrapes. Fear debt like the devil. Be choice in your company. Don't starve yourself to save money for folly, but eat three proper meals a day. Wear wool next your skin. Dishonor no woman. That's all I have to say."

The chaffinch whistled triumph from the garden.

There is little record of what Jean Jacques Audubon accomplished in the studios of David, official artist for the Kingdom, the Revolution, the Terror, the Directory, and the Empire, who in seeking to bring classicism to art created rather a chill pedantry of his own. Audubon says briefly that "David guided my hand in the tracing of objects of large size," but very likely as a young beginner Audubon came only under an assistant's attention. It is hard to imagine what David or his class would have said of a young man who wished to paint birds as they are, when broken columns, velvet draperies, triremes and revolutionaries in togas were the aim of art. "Eyes and noses belonging to giants, and heads of horses, represented in ancient sculpture, were my models," he recorded dryly years later. Of Paris he had nothing at all to say.

Did he throw down his crayon one day and wander to the long window of that studio in the Louvre and look out on the great gray city despairingly?

Was there left in his mind some tiny bright memory of Santo Domingo, the scream of a parrot, or glimpse of little warblers slipping between leaves? Well, Santo Domingo was forbidden to him now; a Frenchman's life was forfeit there since the martyrdom of Toussaint l'Ouverture. And France was going to war with the world. Did he think of Mill Grove, on Perkioming Creek, in far-away Pennsylvania? To all those whom Nature has marked for her own, come irresistible longings for fresh fields, the *nostalgie de partir*. So perhaps it was he who suggested America to his father, or perhaps Captain Audubon was in despair to know what next to do with his son. All that I know is that in 1803 he was in the prow of a vessel as it passed Sandy Hook, and the gulls of America were winging out to greet him.

VI

AT THIS point comes over me the longing to rediscover the America that awaited that ardent French boy. Much is altered, more is gone, and at each spring sign I see or hear, I wonder if he knew it thus. Apart from the tragedy of extinction, there are pulsations in the plant and animal census. It seems to me, for instance, that there were never so many grackles as this spring. Grackles, I know, are the comedy notes; they are not to be encouraged, but the airs would be lonelier without their gabbling and mockery and the sweet squeak and gurgle as of an old mill wheel in a stream. And so much is gone from the woods! When Audubon came, the roar of the passenger pigeons' wings, the harsh call of the Carolina parrot, the drumming of the ivory-billed woodpecker were commonplaces. So too were the tawny hide of the "painter" and the frayed bark of a tree where a young buck had rubbed his horns. It is easy to impoverish a land, sometimes impossible to restore it, and "we do not always know," as an old negro said to me once, "when we are well off until we are poorly."

I have been out to gather a faggot for the fire, and I saw that to every tree spring was coming in a pale green wave, save to the hickories. The borers have got into the shagbarks, and by the look of things their dynasty is ended. It is true, of course, that they are uncouth; they are rigid, scraggly, and their bark is rags. Their leaves, if you like, were always late and dropped early, and if you don't like to work over your nuts, thin-shelled pecans will suit you better. But something is going with the hickories, a thick shell, a brown stain, a grain to turn the blade of an ax, a crude straightness whose place will not be taken by trees like my young elms and ashes.

The morning air was quite glittering with bird song. I heard the first chewinks of the year, and song-sparrows were practising all their different tunes. The bluebird throated his warm warble. And from the edge of the prairies the meadow-larks sang out clear and loud, all wistfulness gone from their voices. On the edge of the slough I stopped, very still in my tracks, to watch two diminutive greenish birds at war in a thorn-apple tree. I was not conscious that there was anything

PLATE LXII

Passenger Pigeon.
COLUMBA MIGRATORIA, *Linn.*
Male 1. Female 2.

PASSENGER PIGEON

else living close beside me except a slim brown bush just out of reach, and I watched the birds, puzzled for an instant over their identity, when suddenly they both told it to me. A tiny crest of red fury was erected upon each head, proclaiming the ruby-crowned kinglet. They teetered and swung at each other, scolding on a note as high and thin as an insect's. It was laughable to see such display of gallantry in the two smallest cock birds in all the woods.

I laughed, and the low brown bush plucked itself out of the marsh, and with dangling legs and outstretched neck became a bittern that departed, uttering its disgusted cry of "Faugh! Faugh!"

As I began to break up the black fingers of a dead oak for my fireplace, I heard the bittern from the next long slough entice me with that contented thumping for which it is called "stake-driver." I sometimes fancy that the bittern likes to be followed about; he could get away a great deal sooner if he really wanted to, but he stands there close beside you, posing with his long neck straight in the air, his eyes on the tip of his bill and his bill pointing straight toward his Creator. The general opinion, says Audubon, is that the bittern so be-

haves from sheer stupidity, but he protests that
he never met a stupid bird.

Of the class of birds called waders, none but
flamingos and ibises strike me as pretty. There
is not a singing voice in the lot of them; their
legs are gangling, their manners are disgusting,
and they dwell in mud and fens where strange
smells arise and there is no footing for humans.
They are the last birds to which the amateur takes
a liking, these coots and rails and herons, snipe
and curlew. You may begin with the thrushes and
hummingbirds, if you are a home-keeping sort of
person owning eaves, vines and a garden, or with
the ducks, if you are a man and an angler and
Nimrod. There are some lucky enough to dwell by
the ocean, and to know where the gannets weave
sea thrift into their nests, to have heard the
"whish!" of the puffin diving and even the sweet
nightly conversation, in their burrows beneath the
sod on the cliff's edge, of the petrels come in from
mid-ocean to nest in sociable colonies. But however you reach the waders, it is a long way round.
They are perhaps the final test of the love of birds,
for one who loves them must be attuned even as
Thoreau, the man who "saw beauty in ashes."
When you come to love them—I do not say it is

possible always to like them—you have got to the last wilderness, you are in the depths of the woods, and ankle-deep in the lost and midmost slough.

I pushed through the door with my bristling faggot, and made the fire. The first crooked blue finger of smoke stole out into the room and brought with it, as odors will, the nostalgia of old happiness that nothing seems to dim. For me there are just two kinds of dwelling—those, like the cabins of our ancestors, where there is always a whiff of woodsmoke, and those others, today a majority, whence it is banished.

I sat down in an easy chair, putting off work, and closed my eyes. I could hear two trains; one, the farther away, blew the long call of warning, softened by distance, that speed and death were on the rails—a glittering train with a name of its own, setting a record pace for a neighboring city that was still so far away that in Europe it would have lain in another land. I could imagine its proud crest of smoke rolled out upon the morning over the black ploughed land. The other train was a freight, and it plodded windily not so very far away, across the prairie beyond the woods; presently it stopped, with a long shuffle, and called a signal at some siding where the frogs would be piping tranquilly from the marsh bisected with the embankment. The engineer—(and where do you see such fine American faces as at the window of a locomotive cab?)—would be leaning out and hearing them, not thinking about them, but about the two white rails ahead, the connected million miles of steel that spiderwebs the continent. There is nothing like a train whistle for taking you everywhere. It makes you homesick for California, or Florida, or Wisconsin or Virginia. Homesick even for home, so far away will it bear you, all in a blast.

So I fell to dreaming on my country, the past and the present indistinguishable. Ox-teams and covered wagons lumbering down a bank between sallows to a ford of the Platte; men going west for gold that most of them would never find. Farmers getting into their Fords in a green twilight, their children hugging their own ribs with excitement, to go to the movies in the town and see people rich as they are rich only on the screen, in cumulative magnificence under the concentrated Kliegs. The Puritan Fathers, writing home about the fertility of New England, the wonderful climate, God's hand over them. The subdivision: lonely pavements and street signs, "Broadway," and

"Rosemount Boulevard"; God's hand over advertising men. Black men and women let up out of the slaver's hold, to look at the palmetto-lined shore they shall inherit. Daniel Boone, blazing death among the antlers and the wigwams of Kentucky. Young men digging today, to put the forests back; billions for relief in a country that could not slay the bison fast enough, that feasted on the tongues and left the carcasses to rot.

This is the land to which came other men, but not Jean Jacques Audubon. Nothing ever really happened to him except birds, for he took nothing else seriously. Even his love affair, his marriage and his home were as those of the birds—a mating for life, a nesting here and there, a foraging by God's grace, a wide roaming and a sure return.

The America to which Audubon came is the bittern and the kinglet, the flamingo and the flicker. I had just myself returned from France and was enjoying my first American spring in many years; I could feel a little what the American forest must have seemed like to that rare company of naturalists who came to these shores, André Michaux, Peter Kalm, Alexander Wilson, Mark Catesby, Alexander Garden, John Clayton, Constantine Rafinesque. The dilemma of an American naturalist in Europe, however delightful his sojourn there, is that there is nothing left for him to find. Every least weed is known and atomized into varieties, encrusted with synonymy, haunted with folklore. The avifauna, though so lovable, is pared down to an attenuation of the great north Asiatic natural faunal province. From tropical Africa, cut off by the Sahara, little may reach it, and that little is hunted. In this our New World, the Linnaean explorers were enchanted with whole new families. And, to feel what they felt, we should very nearly have to stand in the forests of Mars, and hear new cries and see incredible plumage.

The first bird that fell to the gun of Alexander Wilson, nine years before Audubon's coming, as he tramped, a narrow-chested little weaver, from the Chesapeake to Philadelphia, was the red-headed woodpecker, "the most beautiful bird in the world," he wrote home. The wild turkey, the burrowing owl, the whip-poor-will, the cardinal—in the Old World there is nothing like these. The family of the mocking-birds is wholly American, with its catbirds and thrashers. Ours only are the hummingbirds, the vireos, and the gorgeous, black-dashed, whistling *Ictaridae*—orioles and meadow-larks, bobolinks and grackles and redwinged blackbirds. The tanagers are ours, the phoebe and pewee; the two families of warblers keep each to its own side of the Atlantic, and though they are like enough in their habits, they sing to different tunes.

It is the annual wave of migrants from the tropics that gives our bird life its distinction. Its points of resemblance to that of Europe are greatest among our modest permanent residents and the arctic visitants of winter. It was winter still when Jean Jacques Audubon was first installed at his father's estate of Mill Grove on Perkioming Creek that flows down to the Schuylkill River. And I suppose that the icy tinkle of the tree sparrows was the best of bird music around the fine old stone farm house, in the leafless woods of Fatland Ford, a neighboring estate, and all beyond, to Valley Forge, and Gray's Ferry twenty-five miles away where Alexander Wilson was teaching bovine Pennsylvania German youngsters English with a Paisley accent.

As Audubon remembered the circumstances of his coming to America, or as he wished to believe, he had journeyed to our shores as a young gentleman come into his rightful estates—somewhat prematurely at eighteen and with his father still alive to keep a sharp eye on him. Indeed, his father's letters show that the practical Captain did not intend to make an idler of his son; he had sent him to America in the fond hope that he could make a business man of him, and his letter of introduction to Miers Fisher was a request to place the boy in the hands of a respectable American family with sound commercial connections, where he could learn the language and ways of trade.

Friend Fisher, absolutely honest with himself as with the Captain, saw no reason to let the attractive and highly connected young man go any further than his own home. He had a finger in any number of instructive businesses; of English he could teach the boy the godly "thee" and "thy" of the Quakers, and as for the lad's morals, he was sure he had every qualification for guarding them. He opposed fishing, dancing, hunting, violin playing, skating, cards, bird's nesting, skylarking, and youthful high spirits. The boy drank nothing but milk or water, and there remained only the daughters of Eve to fend off. His own daughter offered a solid bulwark against temptation. In short, Friend Fisher had young Audubon's future all arranged for him, from the moment that he fetched him in his carriage from Morristown, where the boy had lain ill with fever in the care of two excellent Quaker ladies.

But when he got his strength back, Jean Jacques saw how the wind was blowing. He took an unreasoning dislike to the gray-clad maiden so frankly put in his way, and fleeing the rule of the meeting house over his habits, he removed himself body and baggage to Mill Grove. Two Quakers of a more liberal persuasion, Friend Thomas and his wife, were his care-takers and his informal retainers. For the first time in his life he was his own master, or at least the leading strings in his father's hands stretched all the way across the Atlantic. He was the squire of broad acres, he had a gun and a dog and a horse and a house of his own. And the birds of America were already on the wing to him from the Orinoco and the Windward Islands, the pampas and the everglades.

The airs of March were icy under the first glitter of the sun; the snow still lingered on the north side of the house and the mill; the roar of the swollen yellow brook was redoubled between its steep clay banks, when Audubon found the cave with the quaint, mysterious little nest fixed in it.

He had no notion who were the owners of this home so cleverly fashioned out of mud and finest

moss, but he had a true naturalist's premonition
that the little architects would return to it. This
was no fragile summer cottage destined to hold a
cup of snow and blow to pieces in the next spring's
winds; some race of birds faithful of heart and
habit had built in the cave, and already his own
heart went out to them. His curiosity, his zeal,
were all alert for the vanguard of the unknown
tribes that would surely come. He went up to his
house and got his books and crayons, his papers
and his gun, and removed them bodily to the cave.
Thenceforward it should be his retreat, and every
day he came there and lingered, standing in the
mouth of the cave where the pale sunlight could
lie upon him, looking south across the faintly bud-
ding maples to a wide fan of sky whence they
would come.

On April 10, 1804, the phoebes returned to
their nest. And in that moment was born the *Ornithological Biography*. Born, too, in Audubon's
mind was that intense curiosity hedged about with
significant doubts that is scientific investigation.
It was an age, we have to remind ourselves, when
the migration of birds was not only scarce understood, but widely disbelieved. Men still followed
Pliny, who thought that the swallow skimming

over the pond hibernated beneath the water like a frog. Barrington, writing to Gilbert White, maintained that British birds would certainly never leave Britain for foreign shores, but fell into a torpor in winter and hid themselves in belfries, caves, and hollow trees.

But Audubon, watching the phoebes repair their home, asked himself by what means a man could be sure that these same little masons found their way over the sea and jungle to one particular spot, for he was convinced that in those tiny gray heads memory and instinct kept the imprint of the great and the small, the continent and the cave. That such a thing should be was nearly miraculous; he would have to find some way of proving it.

So, he says, "I fixed a light silver thread on the leg of each, loose enough not to hurt the part, but so fastened that no exertions of theirs could remove it." His method was so simple that no one else had thought of it. It is astonishing that it did not occur to Gilbert White, who records the finding of a swan bearing on its neck a collar with the arms of the King of Denmark. Alexander Wilson at Gray's Ferry was trying to establish a chain of correspondents, such that not a titmouse or a wren should wing northward but he would know of it. But Audubon was the unconscious founder of the Bird Banding Society that a hundred years later would plot the marvelous course of the plover and the airy track of the bobolink.

Returning from the cave, when the woods were white with bloodroot and the mourning doves were crying contentment in the new-born softness of the weather, he was told, as he pulled off his boots by the fire, that a gentleman had been to call upon him. A Mr. Bakewell, his housekeeper said, the gentleman who had just bought Fatland Ford.

"Oh, yes, the Englishman." Jean Jacques scowled as he dragged the other boot off his foot. "Well, if he comes again, thee shall tell him I am not at home."

"I doubt he will come again, unless thee return his call."

"Little fear that the son of Captain Jean Audubon will pay homage to an Englishman," said the young cock, slipping his feet comfortably into slippers. "Has thee dressed the partridges?"

And he went into the dining-room with the high appetite of youth, the satisfaction of a naturalist who has set discovery afoot, and the obliviousness of one who has not heard the light tap of destiny upon his door.

VII

THE CIRCUMSPECT little nuthatch in her Quakerish dress of neat gray, black and white, peeped around the tree looking upside down at the man, then hid behind the trunk, ran around to the other side and, upon a second inspection, confirmed her startled first impression.

The hunter was dressed in satin knee breeches, silk stockings, elegant pumps, and a ruffled shirt, and the walnut stock of his gun was mounted with chased silver. His long locks flowed gaily to his shoulders; he tossed them as he looked back, whistled, and brought his handsome dog to heel.

"Come along, Zephyr, *mon vieux*. Leave those rabbits—does thee not hear the grouse drumming?"

Men and lands have their golden seasons. Provence in spring, Wordsworth's lake country in June, some say summer in Norway, winter at Karnak, but autumn in America, only in America. Nothing so sad in all the world as autumn

77

north of the Alps, when the leaves fall like tears and lie wet on the pavement, and the mists that rise in the morning do not quite depart all day, to mingle at last with gray twilight. Jean Jacques Audubon had never before seen the Fall, the American Fall, never seen the sumacs wave their orange pinnate banners or the blueberries kindle like a running fire through the woods. Now for the first time he saw our maples burning upward toward the sky, a sky so clear, so blue, so high it went all the way to heaven. He breathed the new tingling air, that smelled of leaf mold and wood smoke and first frost, all shot through with sunshine, and he heard the long torn call of the crows go drifting off through the tops of the tallest trees.

And Jean Jacques was in his golden hour too. He had just reached manhood, as innocent a manhood as even the woods had ever seen. He had all good appetites, no vices, and the most natural vanities. He was gay and he was strong; he rose with the sun and spent the day with the birds. He painted and he hunted, as today he was hunting the partridge and the grouse that melted into the sun-dappled, leaf-strewn forest floor or exploded like a living bomb when Zephyr flushed a covey.

He whistled again, and Zephyr whined warn-
ingly. Jean Jacques peered through the branches,
and a moment later he heard the belling of a
hound, an answer from the pack, and then the
dogs burst out of the thicket and came eddying
around Zephyr and his master, their tails in a
frenzy of signalling. Behind them sounded the
crashing of underbrush beneath boots, and Jean
Jacques grounded his rifle in disgust. If there is
anything worse than meeting a hunter on your
land, it is being encountered on his.

The gentleman who swept his rifle muzzle to the
ground at sight of Jean Jacques was dressed in
the height of hunting style; his boots had a fine
patina of age and polish; his light trousers were
elegantly bagged; a scarlet coat proclaimed him
a foreigner, and from under his shooting cap
looked out a weather-freshened face held high by
a well-tied neckcloth.

"This must be my neighbor, Mr. Audubon," he
said promptly, offering a hand. "Bakewell, sir.
William Bakewell. Get down there, Friar. And
you, ma'am, Juno, down!"

The dogs leaped about between the two men
as they shook hands, all lapping tongues and shining eyes, and Jean Jacques, who certainly knew a

well-dressed man when he saw one, a sportsman when he met one, and a master of his hounds, in that moment forgot how well he had been taught to hate the English. He was swept by that form of envy that carries us straight into ardent friendship, and to the Englishman's courtesy, costume, and perfect pack he replied with a bit of innocent vanity.

"Up, Zephyr!" He snapped his fingers over the silky skull. "And shake hands with the gentleman."

Zephyr arose on his hind legs, walked daintily to Mr. Bakewell, held out his paw and barked once.

Mr. Bakewell chuckled. "Very pretty!" he acknowledged, fondling the dog's ear. "I have heard about you all over the countryside. Your master must have the patience of a mother with you."

"Thee has had patience with me, sir," said the boy with a forthright smile. "Thee called upon me, and I've lacked the manners to return thy call."

"Well, well," said Bakewell forgivingly, "young men have affairs of their own. Here, Friar, here, Juno! That's a deuced fine gun you've got, my boy. Are you a Quaker, that you 'thee' and 'thou' me? Not in satin breeches, I'll be bound."

The talk and the laughter and the whistling to the dogs faded through the woods. The squirrels looked out again, and ran along their highroads through the trees, the wind ruffling their tails.

The gregarious cravings of adolescence had been long delayed in Jean Jacques; they were destined to be singularly ephemeral, but his meeting with William Bakewell had quickened them. With difficulty he made himself wait a day or two so as not to alarm those famous reticences of the English, and when he made ready for his call he took an elaborate care with his dress and hair, and he could have seen his eager young face in his own boots. Mrs. Thomas closed the door upon his departure with a doting chuckle. His sorrel felt the thrill of the frosty morning and he let her have her head, the two dashing as a centaur through the swirls of tumbling leaves.

The mansion of Fatland Ford was imposing; its portico of gleaming columns rose two stories; its classic solidity spoke of gracious living soundly supported by wealth. A negro boy came running to take his horse as he dismounted, and feeling each moment the need of every bit of his finery, and of every grace that was natural to him, he knocked at the broad door.

It was opened at once, and he stepped in. Mr. Bakewell was from home, the servant said; would he care to step into the parlor?

So he went lightly across the polished floor, toward the open doorway and the light of the fire there. He stopped in what at first seemed an empty room, but at the sound of his footsteps Juno arose from the hearth and came towards him, waving her tail, and then from the inglenook stood up a young girl with her embroidery still in her hands and a smile on her lips. Jean Jacques stood bewitched beyond speech or movement.

"My father," said Lucy brightly, "is out. I'll send a servant for him. He'll be so glad you came. Won't you sit down?"

The young man put all his ardor into a bow. "I am Jean Jacques Audubon, thy servant, mademoiselle."

She gave him her hand, tucking the embroidery hoop shyly behind her in the other, and he kissed her fingers.

How beautifully he does that, she thought. Does he guess I'm only fifteen? Do my curls look all right? Are my cheeks as hot as they feel? It's the fire, of course. What a fine brow he has, and how burning his eyes are! But I mustn't stand here like a goose. "Won't you sit down?" she invited again, and took her place demurely by the hearth.

Juno came up, as the young man sat down, and laid her chin yearningly on his knee. His long hand absently stroked her head with an enthusiasm of affection she had never encountered before. His youthful instincts, which had never known a sultry season, awakened now in his eighteenth year, and though his head was in a tumult, his heart had found a steady beat that it would never lose.

This is the opening scene of Audubon's love, as he has frankly told of it. "Well do I recollect the morning," he wrote of it to his sons, "and may it please God that I may never forget it."

When William Bakewell came in, rubbing the cold off his hands, he found his daughter and his young neighbor laughing and talking as famously as old friends. Straddling before the fire, his hands behind him, he cocked his eye at first one and then the other. He saw—a fool would have seen it—how matters stood already, but this young Frenchman was a gentleman as well as a good shot. It really wasn't necessary to believe that

they were all scamps with women and cowards on
the field; and after all, this was America. He regarded his daughter critically; he was a stern dis-
ciplinarian with his children. But he could not but
be proud of her, the good little lass. She was behaving very prettily, not bold, not coy, not unnatu-
ral, but mistress of herself and her father's home.
And, shrewd glance narrowed keenly, he watched
the way the boy looked at her. The young brown
eyes were bewitched enough; there was something
about the fellow's forehead that was candid as
day.

And, for a fact, Jean Jacques would have liked
nothing better than to proclaim his discovery to
Lucy, her father, and the whole wide world. Certainly he did not keep it secret long. His wooing
was open and zealous; as the autumn deepened
into winter, the temperature around Fatland
Ford and Mill Grove seemed to rise. When he had
made a monstrous kill of partridge he had the
whole Bakewell family to dinner, Lucy, her father,
her five brothers and sisters. The boy who had
fancied only "aërial companions" became the gay
young blade. "Not a ball," he remembers, "a skating match, a house or riding party took place
without me."

Love has bloomed upon a moonlit balcony in Verona, under the gas lamps of Limehouse, beneath the twilit elms of Harvard Yard on Commencement night, in a Paris garret, in Wimpole Street, in a Viking feasting hall, and it is, if you like, always the same thing. But it must assuredly taste of a different vintage with each circumstance. To the man under the sky, with his feet upon green earth and the smell of fresh things in his nostrils, sex is a current which seems plainly to be moving in the same direction as his life. He will see sweet and gay faces, delectable figures, with a happy appreciation. But for him there will be but one mate, and if he has not found her yet, he waits. And when she comes, he knows her. For him desire has no poison. It is like the desire of the eyes for light. His thoughts are freer than the wind; he sees the night hours in her hair, the giving in her hands, his children in her arms. For him there is nothing made that may truly adorn woman; only, in the fashions of her day, her womanhood enhances worthless gems or clothes or songs or settings. Of all men he loves furthest from the bestial in man, and most naturally, and to life is most grateful for her, because he cannot tell her from life itself. She is its flower, his need its earth.

So seldom wise in his decisions, Jean Jacques Audubon did not even make the decision to choose Lucy Bakewell. Instinct chose for him, and out of a world of women he found the one perfect girl for him. And when she saw him, she must have seen the whole of him and the truth of him, for she never, in the hard and bewildering years, tried by one gesture to turn him from the strange way he had to go.

VIII

CAPTAIN AUDUBON in his study at La Gerbetière was convinced of two things—that it was a great deal more satisfactory to sail a ship than to become entangled in the knavery of the landsman's moneyed world, and a great deal easier to bring up a maid than a lad with spirit. It was an age when just as a girl was getting difficult to handle you could lay your plans for putting the burden upon another and younger man and know that you had done the best for her. But the problem of Jean Jacques, and of this accursed new-found lead mine at Mill Grove, and all this business of sales, deeds, mortgages and partnerships, rascally lawyers, agents and tenants, merged into one big problem. The Captain picked up his pen, wiped it on the penwiper Rosa had stitched him, and examined the point critically against the light from the gray and doubting French sky. Here were a batch of fresh troubles by letter, to be coped with. The Captain had a poor opinion of

his own ability to express himself or to deal with
these land affairs by correspondence. In this, it
seems, he underestimated himself. His copy book
reveals a man of utmost good sense; his meanings
are perfectly clear, his phrases tactful, his judg-
ments tempered.

He dipped the pen in the well, but he did not
take it out again for a long moment, and his glance
went out of the window to the orangery where
Jean Jacques had played as a child. His thoughts
of childhood's innocence were very tender. But if
his son had lost all his innocence, the Captain
would not have been as troubled as he was now.
Nothing but advancing years and a deepening
sense of responsibility had made of himself the
sort of husband of whom the priest would openly
approve, and when he had planned a sailor's life
for Jean Jacques, he hadn't expected the boy to
be an angel. The alarming thing in the lad's letters was that he claimed to have found an angel.
When under that persuasion, a young man will
defy God as easily as his father, the Captain
knew, and there is nothing for a parent to do but
agree that undoubtedly a head of bewitching curls
and a rustling confusion of petticoats signify a
heart of gold and the purest soul. In the mean-

time, one might take steps. He put pen to paper
and wrote, "To Mr. Dacosta, Philadelphia:"

This Dacosta, in spite of his Portuguese name,
was a man in whom the Captain put a reasonable
amount of confidence. He came of a sound Nan-
taise family. But of course what a man would do
under his neighbors' eyes and how he would be-
have across the ocean were not the same thing.
He certainly gave very full reports upon the lead
mine; the only pity was that the reports were not
better. It was swallowing up money at an ap-
palling rate. Already the Captain had had to split
ownership with Dacosta, and then it had been necessary to turn to his friend, old Rozier, here in
Nantes, place a mortgage on Mill Grove with him
and persuade him to invest sixteen thousand francs
in that bottomless pit of a mine. Little enough of
it all now belonged, for practical purposes, to
the Captain; his share in it, which no one was
inclined to dispute with him, was the responsibility. If the whole venture failed, Rozier would
blame him for getting him into a worthless invest-
ment. If it succeeded, Dacosta and Rozier were
going to have most of the plums. For that reason
he had stipulated that, if luck was with them, Jean

Jacques should be taken into the business with Dacosta.

The Captain, calmly penning measured phrases, was foreseeing the human difficulties that lay in this paper solution. Jean Jacques' letters and Dacosta's belied one another. To be perfectly frank with himself, the Captain suspected that Jean Jacques was least hampered by the truth. But Dacosta too might well be giving way to jealousy of a commercial sort. The Captain, however, had the quarter-deck training; he must uphold his second in command as long as he had any confidence in him at all. He had already written to Dacosta to oppose the boy's match until he, Audubon *père*, was ready to give his consent to it. To put teeth in his disapproval, he had authorized Dacosta to cut off, if necessary, the boy's allowance.

Who were these Bakewells? Did an Englishman leave his country unless he was driven from it? Did they think to repair their fortunes by catching his son with their chit? *Sacré nom*, this would-be father-in-law would find, if he tried any of those tricks, that his daughter was still on his hands, and a son-in-law to boot! Oh, he saw very well how the thing was being done! These contemptible

English played on the boy's vanity, of which he had an overfull measure; they had probably goaded him into boasting that Mill Grove would soon be his. Well, he, Jean Audubon, wasn't going to stand for it. Let them mind lest they burn their fingers!

He put the pen down with an angry satisfaction, and rose to pace up and down his room. This was the least measured letter he had yet written. Not the follies of Jean Jacques, nor the endless complaints of Dacosta had angered him. It was those scheming Bakewells that made him lose his temper. He could see the impoverished *fainéant* father, the minx herself tricked out to catch the boy, and let free to use any art for hurrying up the business. And, *parbleu!* he could see his son too, all too well, strutting and crowing, and billing that little decoy in corners! The Captain struck the back of one hand explosively in the palm of the other. If it weren't for this accursed touchiness in his chest, he would be off for America to send the whole pack about their business.

For a few minutes the Captain gave himself up to behaving like an old-fashioned father. There are molds into which we all flow easily, when we act like all bad boys, all stupid husbands, all complaining old men. But the Captain's individuality soon reasserted itself; he went back to his desk, took a fresh piece of paper, and softened all that he had said. Excuses, mitigations, pleadings.... *My only son ... a boy whose faults are his few years and his impulsiveness. Be patient ... win his confidence by sympathy ... if you are generous with him, he will think of you as his guide and thank you.* It was the point at which a mother would have burst into tears over her letter. It caused the Captain simply to lay down his pen in despair. This was a thoroughly inconsistent missive; one half annulled the other, and he doubted if he would send it.

The dog Médor suddenly set up a tremendous barking in the courtyard. The Captain heard his daughter give an excited scream; there followed his wife's steps running across the terrace. Drawing himself up, he issued from his study, prepared, these days, to deal with almost any eventuality. It was the era of Napoleon's crescendo; there were reports of defeat or victory every day; there were conscriptions, searches, rumors of spies and counter-revolutions; a man's house was scarcely more private than a bivouac.

But emerging from the house, the Captain

heard peals of joy; Médor was yapping in a frenzy of happiness, and there in the garden path stood his son, grown tall and with the winds of travel and wide places about him.

Captain Audubon strode down the garden, and his women folk left off their hysterical demonstrations. He took his son by the shoulders and kissed him on both cheeks, martially. The boy returned the salute with sunny courtesy, but the father with a faint shock sensed instantly that his son was independent, confident, and secretly armed, so that he had already the advantage and was prepared to be magnanimous with his parent.

"Well, my son, your letter announcing your return must have gone down on some unfortunate packet. This is a great surprise for us."

"Surprises are the order of the day," said Jean Jacques lightly, and he tucked his arm through the plump arm of the happily weeping mother, as they all turned toward the house.

Jean Jacques had a moment of sanctuary in his old room. It was chill and clean and much smaller and a little shabbier than he remembered. His mother had bemoaned that it was not ready for him, but he was still elated with the effective surprise he had produced. The door opened, without a servant's formality of a knock, and Rosa came in with a tall pitcher of hot water she had taken from the maid at the head of the stairs. He took it from her hands, saying, "Let's have a look at you, young lady." And he cocked his head on this side and that.

Rosa pirouetted round for him. "Please don't compare me to your Lucy," she said impudently.

"No one is comparable to her," he answered serenely, beginning to wash.

She regarded her brother in love with covert curiosity. "You know, Papa will never let you have her."

"As to that," said Jean Jacques, bringing a wet and shining face up from the basin, "we shall see." He vigorously dried himself and smiled with confidence.

"Well, telling Papa how pretty she is, isn't going to soften his heart," went on Rosa provokingly, and then, coaxing, "but you can tell me all about her."

He tried, and she listened as an expert in these matters. "It's a very mixed up account, my dear," she summed up, "but that's a good sign. I'm sure she's a treasure. But Papa doesn't know—and it was very stupid of you not to tell him—that your sweetheart's people are so well off. You never do think of those things, Jean Jacques."

"I'm not going to tell him," he said rashly. "Not till he's consented first. And you're not to say a word to him either."

"You're an imbecile," said Rosa, but she privately resolved to make the matter public by whispering to her mother.

With her hands behind her she leaned against the big bed post, watching him tie his neckcloth, and making a private comparison of her own. In the mirror he caught sight of his sister's dreaming eyes; he had never seen them so soft before, and he did not flatter himself that his homecoming had put that light there.

"You are in love, too, little sister," he guessed, smiling into her mirrored eyes.

She dropped her lids and laughed.

"How do they take that on the quarter-deck?" he inquired.

"Oh, Papa approves," she said demurely.

"But shall I?" he demanded with mock sternness.

"You'd better. Gabriel's your superior officer."

"Gabriel? Not old du Puigaudeau! Why, the lucky old fox! The blessed young scamp!"

"Oh, Jean Jacques, isn't he wonderful?"

"Never saw anybody like him!" said Jean Jacques solemnly, and then he burst into laughter, clapped his hands to her waist and danced her around the room.

Dinner was not without its constraints. A warm bond of transient sympathy between the boy and girl brought them into an unspoken alliance against their elders. Madame Audubon fluttered distracted as a pigeon, between two loyalties. The Captain confined himself to remarks such as "What boat did you come in, sir?" "Who was the Captain?" "This wine is corked, Annette." "Rosa, take your elbows off the table."

"I sailed on the *Hope*, sir, out of New York, January eighteenth, I think it was. Did you ever sail under a love-sick captain? Ours had just got married and was in no mind to go to sea. So, after he'd passed Sandy Hook he had the carpenter bore holes in her hull and of course we had to put in at New Bedford for repairs. That's where his turtle-dove lived. We lay a week there, while they nested."

Rosa and he both laughed heartily. Their parents were silent.

"But I'll say this for the Captain," the boy

went on. "When we had anchored at Paimboeuf, this morning, and the good fellow heard you sailed under the flag too, he had me put ashore by a special launch. And so, *me voilà!*"

The Captain allowed the ladies to withdraw before he poured himself a glass of dessert wine, and addressed himself to his son.

"Well, my boy, what did you come back for? It's a very bad time to be in France. I doubt if I can save you from conscription."

"I had to come back, Father. Your interests are going to the devil in America, and they're keeping it from you."

"So-ho!" the Captain said, putting up one eyebrow. "You're making a very serious charge there. I wonder if you've had enough experience to know that you're right?"

"Of course I know," Jean Jacques said, leaning across the table. "Everybody in Philadelphia knows it. That lead can't be sold for the cost of uncovering it. And Dacosta has found that out, even though he doesn't know a blessed thing about mineralogy, as he pretended."

"Then what's he going on with it for?"

"To get more money out of you and Monsieur Rozier. Oh, his accounts add up very neatly on the surface. He's an accomplished accountant, at least."

"'I've placed every confidence in him."

"So you have, *mon père*. But who has your resources more at heart, Dacosta or your son?"

The Captain, not without shame, put out of his mind the possibility he had considered that Jean Jacques was moved by jealousy or resentment.

"So you have come back to denounce him?" he asked.

"Indeed I have. He is a covetous wretch and the most shameless swindler that ever lived. Why, do you know, he cut off my allowance and swore it was by your orders!"

His father had privately to swallow another mouthful of brine.

"Altogether, you haven't much to say for him," he advanced cautiously.

But Jean Jacques was magnanimous. "He's intelligent," he allowed, thinking privately that Dacosta had praised his bird drawings and predicted that he might become a great American naturalist.

"How did you get the money to come over?" asked the Captain.

"Yes, how indeed! Not from Dacosta, you may be sure. When I told him I wanted to come back

here, he knew his game was up. So he gave me a
letter of credit to New York. I walked all the
way—I was so furious I almost ran—and when
I got there I took it around to this Kauman fellow of his. When he read it, he just laughed. What
do you think it said, Father? That I was to be
arrested and shipped to Canton!"

"No, by thunder!" Captain Audubon thumped
the table. "But they couldn't do that!"

"So they found out. But Dacosta was desper-
ate; he'd have tried anything. So Mr. Benjamin
Bakewell in New York loaned me my passage in
the *Hope*."

"*Ah, oui, ces Bakewell.*" The Captain tasted
his wine thoughtfully. "Well, I shall reimburse
this gentleman, of course."

"I knew you would, Father. He's a very fine
man. The brother of Mr. William Bakewell."

"Who is the father of Lucy," suggested the
Captain.

Sunlight broke in Jean Jacques' face. "Of
Lucy," he confirmed. "*Mon père,* she is the one
girl I want to marry."

Captain Audubon looked anxiously at his son's
face, for traces of the girl there. What he saw

he admitted inwardly, was sincerity. And for the third time he was ashamed.

"Well, now, my son," he began, "you are deeply in love, I can see that. I am willing to believe that you would not love beneath yourself."

"Dacosta said the Bakewells were beneath us," broke in Jean Jacques. "But it's not true at all. They are very fine people; even you wouldn't be able to help liking them. They're cultivated and generous; they have brought up Lucy like a little princess."

The Captain accepted these facts with an outward "Hm," though he was secretly delighted to re-arrange his conception of the Bakewells. "But I was not thinking only of that side of it. Women —girls—are divided into classes by their souls, not their social position. I am willing to believe, I say, that of a woman's soul you are as good a judge as I." He saw the flash of his son's affectionate smile, and avoided it in his glass. "So much for love. We come to the matter of marriage. When young folk are wed, they link two families; they found a third. It is a serious business—takes co-operation, compromise. Many people and their affairs are concerned. What has Mr. Bakewell to say to this matter?"

"He says," Jean Jacques got out painfully, "that I shall have to show how I shall make my way in the world before I may have Lucy."

"I am beginning to think rather better of this Mr. Bakewell! I have helped you in every way I know how, Jean Jacques, and I shall continue. But if you want this young lady enough, you will win her." He stood up, and the boy rose too.

By a word here, a look, a tone of voice, the household knew within the hour how the land lay. Jean Jacques had denounced a scoundrel to his father, served the family fortunes, and opened the doorway for his love affair. His mother congratulated him only with a warm embrace; young Rosa was jubilant. But Jean Jacques abruptly put aside her chatter. He went to his old room and closed the door. The elation of return and victory was over, and suddenly he did not wish to be a hero among women. True, it was sweet, here in France; he was not wholly sorry that he could not at once return to America. His childhood home gave him a moment's refuge in childhood.

But he saw that going back was a final thing, when he should have to stand against the world. Another young man, say, Ferdinand Rozier, the old merchant's son, born with a head for business and a heart for it as well, was merely entering into life, from it to wrest its recognized prizes. But to Jean Jacques the obstacles towered high as the Himalayas, and without wings he did not see how he could get over them. In that moment he experienced real humility. He envied his father, whose love of the sea was yet a love that could be turned to account; he envied du Puigaudeau, whose duty was to obey and draw a salary for it. There was an obedience for Jean Jacques, but in the impending encounters he would not be bowing to it. For it is the dilemma of genius that whether you follow your own calling or walk in the ways of other men, you have to do the hardest thing in the hardest way.

He went to the window and pushed it open upon the chill twilight, a sad, doubting hour; there is nothing like it in the New World, where the weather is either good or bad. But this month at the mouth of the Loire was not winter or spring, but some cautious and compromising date without hopes and without birds. His thoughts flew west, and they winged around the woman—for to him she was complete and perfect—that he loved. His picture of her at that moment was so intense, something so projected upon the consummations of the future, in the privacy of some imagined wilderness, that longing overcame him like a mounting fever. He closed the window, went unsteadily to his bed and flung himself there with his face in his arms, his solitary heart beating in his own ears.

IX

IT TAKES many years and perspective on our own words and actions to make us sincerely generous about our enemies, but Audubon, after the lapse of decades, shows in his memoirs how much he still hated Dacosta. Even so, I doubt the man was quite as black as Audubon painted him. At that moment in his life Jean Jacques must have been a young handful, and the lead mine never did pay under any one's direction, though so astute a man as Stephen Girard is said to have been interested in it.

Dacosta was rather the sort of man we were looking for in those days, an energetic capitalist who would bring money and intelligence into the country and turn to account the slumbering wealth of the land, that had been wasted by God upon heathen savages. Up to twenty years ago we were still welcoming the immigrant, even though he came penniless. We could actually offer him the fabulous possibility that twenty years after he stepped in broken shoes upon Manhattan, he might be a baron of, say, the white pine trade, and that at a wave of his hand wooden cities would spring up, railroads would be bent to him, fleets would be built for him, and the stock markets would sicken at the mere rumor of some access of his temper.

Or even suppose that he neglected what a distinguished American historian has called the national virtue that transcended all other morality— the virtue of prosperity; he was still welcome as a man, one more American in the census. The immense pioneer families were not purely accidental; a farm, like a fort, needs numbers, and every pioneer household was both. Women were called upon to supply this national man power, and children were conscripted by their conception into the frontier army.

For we had a void to fill; the paradise of Kentucky in 1760 seems to have been almost empty even of Indians. And a void cannot exist when no wall separates it from a plethora. Europe pressed upon America; the Atlantic states pressed upon the Northwest Territory. The will of emperors or dictators could not have held back that great wave, and if the Ohio Valley had still belonged to

New France, the Americans would by no will of their own have poured into it and wrested it away. We took Texas and California by violence; perhaps we only paid for Louisiana because Jefferson bought it before the Americans got there.

These facts can be restated in other ways that sound better and are also true. "Manifest destiny" was the phrase we used for it then. Even the violence may be excused. Our movement was fore-ordained by history. The invention of the astrolabe by the Arabs enabled Columbus to steer a course across the Atlantic. The steps from 1492 to the capture by treachery of Osceola, who came out to meet the Americans under a flag of truce, are inevitable. We happened, at that moment, to be shamefully in the wrong. But Indians are treacherous too. New Spain was treacherous.

It is the spiritual history of countries that historians so seldom write. I am not suggesting that I think that lands that have neglected their material advancement for mysticism, contemplation and fatalism are better to live in or more to be admired. Speaking practically, spiritual health is most manifest in a country where the sanctity of human life is first regarded, where thought and speech and mode of living are matters of liberty, where peace is the ideal, and the ant and the cricket, the coal miner and the ballet dancer, are not compared one to the disadvantage of the other, but both accepted and repaid.

In the era that our historians call the "period of good feeling," meaning that we were united in our hatred of England and had not yet aroused our consciences to slavery, we were a stirring spectacle of a young nation; there is no American of old stock who cannot feel the pull of those days, a great longing for their gusto, their possibility and adventure.

But what about the spiritual health of that nation? How sacred was human life then? Did we want peace, if it meant that we couldn't have what we wanted more? Could you question slavery in Charleston, argue the rights of the factory worker in Rhode Island, lean towards popery in the Back Bay? Could you declare yourself in your speech and dress a foreigner, without arousing mirth or suspicion? Could you seriously propose to spend a life studying and painting the birds? It was a moment when one man could not stand out against a multitude, when for Jean Jacques there was little to do but to conform. Or to seem to conform; the herd is satisfied with appearances.

So Jean Jacques became John James Audubon, earnest citizen of the young republic, a clerk in the exporting and importing house of the excellent Benjamin Bakewell in the city of New York. The position was only intended to be temporary, a training for the firm of Rozier and Audubon, its wise heads in Nantes, its young limbs, John and Ferdinand, in the New World.

The twenty-nine-year-old Ferdinand was also clerking it, in Philadelphia, in order to learn English. Lucy had polished off John's, quaintly larded as it was with Quaker and French idioms and accents. So now, against the dusty squares of the office window, framing a glimpse of masts and sails, behold John James translating Mr. Bakewell's letters for the good Rozier of Nantes and worrying about gloves and wines from France, coffee and indigo from America. But his heart is at Fatland Ford and his head is with the birds.

Of the New York of 1806-7, Audubon complained that it had entirely too many people in it. The noise and bustle he found frightful. But the New Yorkers had something to say against Audubon. Neighbors complained of the odors issuing from his lodging where, at night and of a holiday, he was stuffing and mounting specimens. He

worked thus in odd moments for the eminent Dr.
Samuel Mitchell, scholar, senator, physician and
naturalist. When he was free he roamed the
vicinage of New York for water birds; the harbor,
New Jersey and Long Island, with their marshes
and strands, are even today a happy hunting
ground. And when time pressed, he found his
models in the market; it was a day when birds
now rare or well-nigh extinct were offered for a
trifle in the city stalls.

But the undiscovered empire of the birds lay to
the west, beyond the Alleghenies that walled in the
thirteen settled states. There was the great basin
where were collected the waters of the continent,
the trough of the mightiest bird migrations. Those
who had penetrated to Kentucky and the Old
Northwest would tell you that if you had not seen
sycamores of Ohio, bur oaks of Illinois, and cypress of Kentucky, you had not seen trees. It is
hard to realize this now when the Middle West
stands for a profitable platitude, but the Middle
West was unknown in the days of Audubon and
Boone, unknown as a name and as the human and
mental province that it now is. It was then Farthest
West, and the thought of it excited the national
mind. Thoreau on his rocky acres was to compare

the richest fields of the imagination to Ohio soil.
When Alexander Wilson had spied out every wren
and tit, he yearned for fabled Transylvania, for
the falcons and cormorants, the pigeons and the
loons of the great central swamps and forests.
Wonder tales were rife in those days, of Mammoth
Cave, of poor men who gave their every child a
bearskin blanket and a coonskin cap. Of black loam
a mile deep, of antlers proud as trees. Of strange
mounds like great serpents, work of some mysterious vanished people. The wilderness, waiting
for the man who would love it most.

He came to it, disguised as a business man, merchant trader, of the firm of Rozier and Audubon.
He came alleging his purpose to be commerce. He
offered axes, and shotguns, powder horns and
calico to the men and women who were rolling back
the frontier with a speed which has never been
equalled since God made the world and found it
good as it was. At Louisville, then a rough settle-
ment of barely a thousand people, Audubon and
Rozier set up a shop.

So here he was, in at the beginning of a future
metropolis, and from the look of things there was
no reason why he should not become in Louisville
what Astor was in New York, or Field in Chicago,

an empire builder, a pioneer of big business. He was facing front; he was in step and marching with the vanguard. For the moment he enjoyed the sweet and really very inexpensive taste of other men's approval.

In the thorn-apple trees the mourning doves complained and in the hickories the jays screamed mockery. John James Audubon arranged his goods on shelf and counter, his back to the door. They had said he must show his worth in the world before they would give him Lucy. He measured off his ells of cloth, he weighed his pounds of tea, he counted his coins into the till and totted up his ledger. The meadowlarks told him how sweet the first spring sun was, and the cardinal called "Hurry, hurry, hurry! Quick, quick, quick!" But John was earning Lucy.

And in April of the year 1808 he came to claim her.

There were reasons enough, from Miss Blakewell's point of view, against this marriage, and I don't doubt there were kind friends who urged them. But Miss Bakewell and Lucy were not really the same person. Her mother was not living, and the intense dislike which her new stepmother took to Audubon was not very likely to sway Lucy, un-

less it made her dislike her stepmother. Her brother
Thomas was Audubon's ardent admirer, her small
sister Eliza's head was full of the romantic drama
of a wedding; as for William Bakewell, her father,
he had so far become an American that he asked
chiefly that his daughter should be pleased with
her own choice. He had the wisdom to recognize
the inevitable. Against the great simplicity of the
love of these two young people, no amount of reasons, however good, could stand.

I think he came to get her when April was a
day old, and they rode off together, she English-
fashion and he astride; and when her horse bent
down its head to put a soft muzzle in the brook
still running icy, he got down and gathered her
blue hepaticas with their dark true leaves. Then
they went on, to Mill Grove and past the old mill
itself, to the cave, and they dismounted. They left
the two beasts to crop what greenery they could
find, and went in, each saying with his heart to
the other, "Do you remember? Do you remember?"
For—(and I am happy at this)—it was in the
phoebes' retreat, five years ago, that he had sat
at her feet and spoken up into her eyes and she
had nodded, turned away her head and given him
her two hands that he put his face in.

Now he threw his coat across the boulder seat, and she sat down, and he came behind her and bent down and kissed her hair and her brow, tipping her face back, his hands cupping its oval.

"Only a week more," he said.

"Then what?" she teased.

"Thee knows." With his Lucy he still used the Quaker form of address, the only equivalent he could find for the tender *tu*.

"Thee and I," she mocked him, "shall stand up before the Reverend Doctor Latimer from Philadelphia, and every one will look at thee, and thee will be very uncomfortable, and I shall be very happy and complacent."

"Every one will look at *thee*," said Audubon. "It is droll, that, about Doctor Latimer, his being an Episcopalian, when my mother had me baptised a papist and thy father is a Unitarian."

"Who cares?" said Lucy. "I think the service in the English church is the most beautiful, don't you?"

"Doctor Latimer may speak Choctaw for all I shall hear it," her lover promised.

"So much, then, for a week hence," said Lucy. "But what about the years, John?"

He released her, and looked out of the cave's

mouth as if he could discover what was winging toward them through those years. She waited, looking at him. Her eyes were very level under her dark arched brows. I think she saw what time would bring her, for if it was written already that birds were his destiny, she was already wise with the knowledge that her destiny was John. Whatever he did, whatever became of him, she wanted only to be there, where he was, his mate.

He turned back and took her hands, and he looked at them and not at her eyes, as he said, "We'll make a home in Louisville; business is going there, and Rozier's got a head for money. Thee will get to like him better, dear; it's just that he hasn't any way with women at all."

She shook her head. "He doesn't appreciate you, John."

"Oh, come now! We're just in business together. I'm a terrible fellow to get on with, and he sounds a lot warmer in French. Our families are old friends, and they've signed and sealed us up together in a pact only less binding than marriage."

In her intuitive breast, the girl knew that pacts are worthless when hearts and personalities pull apart. She felt that, all unconsciously, Rozier was the enemy of her John's future, though he was so honestly laboring to further it. She deflected their talk from the subject.

"And Louisville," she asked, "what shall I find that like?"

John warmed to this topic. "It's small," he said, "but choice. Settled by Virginians, mostly; some very fine women; the men are all sportsmen. And everybody has money to spend for the things we need to sell them. There will certainly be friends for us there. There's even a French family—Nicholas Berthoud. His mother's a remarkable old woman; she was *dame d'honneur* to Marie Antoinette. My Lucy won't be wholly among savages."

"I shan't be wholly with any one but you."

"No, it isn't the others that matter," he said, looking at her now. "I'd rather there was not another soul but us in all Kentucky. Just thee and me in the wilderness, and my crayons and my violin."

"What should we do in a world without other people in it?" she laughed. "Who would come to buy at your store?"

"Why should I need to keep a store then? We should live upon turkey and quail and venison, and

I would cover thee with a bear's skin and make
thee shoes of the fawn's hide, and find thee the wild
bees' honey. And paint for thee the whistling
swan."

She looked at him tenderly, as if he were a
child. And he bent the same regard upon her, for
as she sat there daintily in her flowing skirts,
her fine gloves in her lap, her hair rippling neatly
about her head, the Bakewells of Castle Donning-
ton looked out from her face. He imagined this
child of wealth beside the roaring, tawny Falls of
the Ohio. He remembered the lean, sallow cabin
women of Kentucky, thrice mothers at her age.
And he looked ahead to the wooden walls of the
forest, and wondered how he could cut a path for
them there.

Because he did not know the answer he kissed
her, and she put her arms around him, less seek-
ingly than to assure him. As a bird takes the air,
leaving the nest where it was fledged, the small
dear radius it has learned, to seek far places it
has never seen, so Lucy faced the westward journey into life, buoyant and deeply certain.

The week sped round; the windows of Fatland
Ford blazed with the wedding candelabra of John
and Lucy; the fashionable Doctor Latimer arrived

SELF-PORTRAIT OF THE ARTIST, IN MINIATURE

in his carriage from Philadelphia, with his purple ribbon in the right place in his prayer book. Mr. Bakewell was irascible with the willing servants; the child Eliza made herself small in corners and missed nothing; and Mrs. Bakewell did her best to put a face upon an occasion which she regarded as most lamentable. Lucy, peeping from the drawn curtains of her bedroom window, saw her radiant brother leap down from a carriage, followed by John. Instantly she drew back. The negress Tertullia came forward with the wedding gown in her hands, and the slip of bare-armed girl in her petticoats disappeared forever in the torrent of silk. When she emerged, she was already a bride, flushed and expectant.

She sat at the dressing-table to have her hair rearranged and it seemed to her that the black fingers were an eternity about it.

"Oh, never mind any more," she said impatiently, and as Tertullia continued to fuss over her, she rose and drove her laughingly out of the room.

Then for a moment she stood alone, listening to the commotion and the babble of gladness in all the rooms below. How shall I tell it, that moment when a maiden takes leave of herself? Men do not know of it; women do not talk of it.

Without a knock, Eliza burst into the room, her eyes dancing, and music rose up the stairs on wings behind her.

"They're all waiting! Mama says you're to come down. Oh, Lucy, how beautiful you look!"

The bride bent down to her and took the child in her arms, hugging through the frills to the little firm core of her.

"Goodbye, dear," she said, and kissed the soft places in her neck.

"Goodbye?" cried the child in uncomprehending dismay.

The music called imperiously. Lucy freed herself from the tightening thin arms, and stood up straight. She walked to the head of the stairs, her hand upon the polished rail, and with a small slippered foot she took her first step forth. From the bottom of the flight shone up John's golden smile. And all beyond him lay the wilderness.

X

THE WORLD has always been ragged with wilderness, but every one can feel the difference between that in which John the Baptist went crying and this one to which John James brought his Lucy in 1808. Where John the Baptist strode with long hair and uplifted hands, there had been many prophets before him; wherever the jackals run there have been cities once, and part of the dust was bones. The jungle too is wilderness, with a life so intensely its own that it will efface you, your step and your seed. Jungle and desert sands will take care of themselves; men have small odds against them. The North American wilderness, whether forest or prairie, was unique in being the last of the temperate zone that was virgin. It is that virgin with which we Americans are still in love.

In the day when those two lovers vanished west into the forest, America was in her Homeric age. We still teach its epic to our children, even while we borrow our culture from the east. We still feel when we go to Europe that it is our Persia, and to each traveler she holds out some different sort of treasure. She will enrich the mind and the senses, but we cannot decently lose ourselves in her, and there comes a moment when we lay down everything she has given us to look at and love, because we have to go back home, unable to explain. You cannot explain how you might want Lake Superior when you were living on Lake Maggiore, or why you might be homesick for Sweetwater when you could consort with the ghosts of the Dorias at Dolceaqua. Foreigners cannot come to our Nature as we can come to England's through her poets. Keats' *Ode to a Nightingale* is Keats (and there is no higher praise) but it is not a nightingale. Even when you hear it sing, you cannot get free from civilization. The magic of that voice—and there is no question that it is the most marvellous tone that ever escaped from bird throat—derives in part from the haunting sense of the past and all we know of other men who have listened to it.

In America our past is not so pervasive, and it is never oppressive. Our wide airs have scarce been breathed before. Our mandrake does not, like the

European plant of which it is namesake, grow even in fancy under gibbets to catch dead men's blood; it is simply a flower. Our wild grapes, so honeyed sweet in bloom, so untamed and tart in fruit, do not make me think of Bacchus or a drunken nymph; they are only wild grapes and part of the woods. Our hawks have never been hooded, and no Shelley has written an ode to our meadowlark. The European mind feels these lacks. Our Nature is not literary, it is not historic, it is not ethnological—you may except what associations the Indian had with Nature, but where are they now? In Smithsonian reports, but not in my woods. The primate species that entertained them is gone from the fauna. It is not that we are too young a nation to have humanized our Nature; we shall never do so. The white man came to America ten thousand years after he came to Europe; he came with the gun and the plough. He came with a belief in a single invisible God, so there was nothing to fear, nothing to propitiate, and for him there was no nymph behind an echo, no sprite in the bog lights, no king of the elves beneath the mountain.

We like this as we have it. We are proud of being free of the saints and the satyrs. Our air seems very clear to us. At least we see our wild life through a pane of clear glass. How much of it is left for you and me depends a little upon our geographical good fortune. It is possible to do marvels, of course, in the tamest parochial environment; look at Thoreau, who seldom left Walden Pond. But he said himself that the scene was emasculated. Some God-given bounty is no more.

I sloshed out this morning to the cabin in the woods, and in the first long slough a sandpiper was nodding and pacing; he flew off at the sight of me with strong sweeps of his pointed wings. In the second slough something big with rushing pinions flung the water about and startlingly ran up on the land and lost itself, unnamed. I went on through the groves of bur oak where the mandrakes were opening out their umbrellas. The third slough is a lake, and by now I knew that if I stole to it cautiously a third and strangest bird would be there. I had the advantage, for I could approach it across boggy ground where no twig snapped under my feet and no leaves rustled, and the screen of the willows hid me. I no sooner had a good view of the lake, a silvery, languid sheet with cat-tails making a jungle of one end, than I saw the wild duck. It was solitary and contented; it sailed about into the sudden wind riffles and out of them, turning its tufted head serenely to regard the watery world. Once or twice it spoke to itself, a low, scolding quack.

It was not a beautiful duck; it was gray with a somewhat fantastic ruddy topknot. But the reality of Nature (and the wilderness was its supreme reality) is not esthetic. Audubon's Kentucky was not esthetic. I doubt if Eden was; it was unselected, generative, inconceivably abundant. So Kentucky depended on nothing man could bring to it; it was either hostile to man or it died under his hand. The ducks, the *Anatidae*, precisely point my contention. Of all birds there is most wild about them; the marsh, the rain, the torn sky, the flight, the whistling commands—these give to them the fatal allure of the things that flee and are most gallant in the face of death.

So this merganser rose upon a whistling of stiff plumage, leaving a silver wake upon the water, and in the style that fowlers love so well, she turned, low in the air, and wheeled past me to the right, offering a perfect mark. I felt the sportsman's thrill, and was glad I had no gun. I only watched as with lowered neck she made off across the boglands to the distant river or a farther lake. This style of flight is what the hunter means when he says the duck furnishes good sport, and if they were unpalatable I think he would still shoot at them. But it is not only the sportsman, even with such a vile abuse of the duck's confidence as the practice of baiting, that has thinned their ranks; it is what we do to their breeding grounds. Model agriculture drains the marshes where they feed; it grubs out and burns off the bushland where they nest. And the mere presence of civilization affrights them, so that in truth they die at our touch; we are all of us slayers of the wilderness, helpless participants in its destruction. Until today a single gray merganser is a stranger here, one flake of the wilderness descended into my woods.

In the twelve days of their wedding journey to Louisville, by flatboat down the Ohio River, John and Lucy Audubon saw more water fowl than I suppose I shall ever see. It was spring, and the ducks and the wild geese were fleeing from that soft, flowery southern warmth, passing overhead in a crying, wheeling crowd for the north where, on the fir-ringed lakes, in the marshes and the bogs, they went to mate in the brief, sweet weeks of the arctic summer that is all one day. The Ohio, then, was a world of wings, of water and islands and shores with the forest marching down to the brown strand where giant driftwood lay. Only here and there a farm, smoothing the contours of the land, swept down with generous furrows to the water. With each hundred of miles the farms grew fewer, and only a squatter's cabin here and there betrayed itself by a blue spiral of smoke rising above the forest crown.

The craft in which they floated through this innocent Eden was called an ark, and Audubon writes of these vessels that they accommodated the immigrants, their wives, children, cows, sheep, pigs, dogs, cats, chickens, ducks and geese; on the deck were piled beds and bedding, farm implements, spinning wheels and stoves. But he must have been lucky in the ark in which he carried off Lucy, with a few other young couples, for of that journey he records no discomforts.

When the voyagers were in need of meat, they made fast to the bank, and in a few minutes the men would have teal and turkey and grouse enough for a feast. The women had built the fire and found a spring, and soon the spit was turning, and the odor of woodsmoke and browning fowl mingled with the smell of fern and lichen and moss. Then as twilight closed, and Venus stole forth in the west, the travelers would fall silent, gazing across the majesty of the winding river that caught the last of the afterglow. A boatsman's horn wound faintly from among the islands, and near at hand the nighthawks swooped along the shore, pursuing insects in the last of the light. When darkness came the whip-poor-will calling in the depths of the forest brought eeriness to the moment, and the couples, hand in hand, went back to the ark, where in the prow John took his fiddle under his chin and drew a sweet bow across the responsive strings.

Before daylight, as they drifted asleep down the pale river, began the singing in the wilderness. Voices calling to their mates moving silently in the gloom between the very young leaves of April. First little twitterings and whistlings, a tentative trying of sound in the deep silence. Then the mourning dove, who does not mourn but is content. Then the young cheer of the robins; then the rattle of the flickers and kingfishers, and just before the sun rose from the arms of the trees, the three twirled notes of the wood thrush, so tempered in its gladness. The glittering began; the light pierced in smoky shafts through the forest damp; it danced upon the river ripples, was a

blade edge on every leaf, was a diamond sparkle
in the dew upon the spider webs. And the great
chorus broke forth. The cardinal shouting "Pretty,
pretty, pretty!" The concert from many brown
thrashers, all the singing sparrows and their many
little tunes, drumming from the woodpeckers, flut-
ing of the orioles, a run of happy tanager notes,
song and song and song.

So passed the honeymoon journey, the oddest,
surely, in the unwritten history of lovers—a wild
ride over the mountains by coach, almost a thousand miles by winding river where we may guess
that on that little boat the bride lay down among
other women, and the eyes of her lover were half for
the birds. But all manner of strange things might
happen in those times in Kentucky and on the Ohio.
Johnny Appleseed in sack cloth, without shoes to
his feet, rafting it down from Fort Pitt with seeds
of apple by the peck. Tom Lincoln and his Nancy
a-courting, and a damn fine girl, sir, even if he
didn't know who her father was. Runaway lovers
from Carolina, the woman riding pillion, her
fearful gaze still searching the pines behind them.
Whole families removing wealth, slaves, ancestral
portraits, Chippendale and silver, from Virginia.
Outlaws, long-rifles, restless men, misfits, land

speculators, Indian fighters, Indian cheaters, pearl fishers. Robert Owen founding a perfect socialist state at New Harmony on the banks of the Wabash. Methodists already holding revivals under the trees. Here and there a lonely priest, a lonely Jew, a circuit dancing teacher, a rare naturalist, Rafinesque at Lexington, Thomas Say at New Harmony. And Boone, of course, if you admire him. But out of that multitude there were only two, for me, these two upon the stubby prow of the ark as it noses the last miles down to Louisville.

In the small chill breeze that had sprung up with sundown, she nestled in the warmth of his strong right arm. He stood bare-headed to the wind, and it played with his long locks and lifted them from his shoulders. She had borne with this odd and strenuous honeymoon like a lady, even when the coach upset in the Alleghenies and she was painfully bruised, but in secret she was glad that it was ending. For that end would be her beginning, the branch at last after the long flight. She knew how he loved her; she had thought she knew how he loved the birds, but she had not guessed how they could take him away from her.

"You have been happy," she said.

But he did not tell her how happy; he spoke only as her lover when he answered, "We shall be happier, thee and me, when we have our own home. It's a fair land and a rich one, and we shall grow with it. I can see a house there, outside of the town, thy gardens and thy servants. And Rozier," he chuckled, "with a wife, I hope, to keep him busy—on the other side of the town."

Lucy did not laugh. All this was sensible to expect. It was but loyalty in a wife to see, in her young husband just set up in business, the prosperous merchant of later years who would bring to her all that he now promised. And yet—nor was it because John's very first venture, a fling in indigo, had already failed to the tune of several hundred pounds—Lucy could not really see, did not in her heart believe, in that future man of substance with his house and lands and servants of which she was to be mistress. That was not John. And it was John she wanted. It was this hour that she wished would last for a lifetime, this little hour while John's arm was all her shelter and the wooded horizon their only walls, the river their open door, and the wind of the future blowing into their faces. A wind with the last thin ice of the passing winter on the edge of it, and all the sweetness of the small flowers opening in the woods. She drew it deep into her lungs, this wilderness air that was his element, and she could feel it entering into her blood and altering it, so that change ran secretly in her veins.

She did not stir in the curve of his arm, and yet the woman he held was growing; however great he might become she was to be of a stature to match him. She was a girl now, and their prospects were all rosy, but she was wise and read her own womanhood and foresaw how it would bend, freighted, as the years ripened. No elder woman awaited her in this new land, with comforting and counsel; if she was to have a home, it must be of her own making; the man beside her, perfect in love was, she knew well, imperfect in his wisdom.

The darkness had stolen down now out of the forest, out of the sky, to close about the palely shining river. And suddenly a great horned owl swept across the boat's prow, so close it fanned her face with the deathy wind of the hunt. He drew in his breath with sharp pleasure, and caught her close for reassurance.

"I am not afraid," said Lucy quietly.

XI

NOW THE idyll is ended. Now is boyhood finished, now the tone deepens. Now the soft clay goes
to the wheel. A very strange vessel is molded of
it; the glaze upon it is fair enough, but how odd
the shape, and what can be the use of it? Here the
strong hands of the frontier have compressed and
heightened it, and the Frenchman has been pulled
awry into the form of the backwoodsman with a
fondness for practical jokes, with the marksman's
dropped lid, the fowler's pride in a full bag. Here
is the idler, the whittler, the tale-teller drawing a
longer bow than Robin Hood. The wanderer, the
man who, hating to hear his neighbor's cocks crow,
must always move on into a newer country. He
has a curly mouth, like Lincoln's, the shoulders
and hair of a Boone, and most of his pictures
show him with a gun, like Crockett. A van Winkle
mixed with a Charlevoix. Not a trace of an Astor
or a Field, after all; rather you might think him
one of those thousands who, individually failing

of wealth or power or any sort of greatness, made up the composite greatness of the old frontier. But wait. There is a thumbprint upon the clay of the vessel, from no human hand. Not all the forces of history, of destiny, of empire, leave that grand original sign that no man can forge.

Louisville, on its benches and doorsteps, in its drawing-rooms where ladies sit together, on its wharves and over its counters, passed him a thousand times in review. *I wouldn't be that partner of his; leaves him to mind the store, while he's off bird's-nesting.... He's a damn fine shot, and he'll drive you a nail into a tree at fifty paces.... He's mighty well spoken, good company on a hunt.... Such a divine dancer, my dear, but would you really like to be his wife? Their money won't last long, you know, and he's off from her, in the woods, for days. And no knowing when he'll turn up for meals. But there, he's the kind of man that thinks he can make it all up to you with a kiss. Perhaps she thinks so too. She isn't discontented; she's prouder of him than if he were Bonaparte. And she looks at you, when you say something about him, in a straight sort of way, and keeps her thoughts to herself....*

A CHILD'S VOICE: He gives me sugar when I go

in the store. He thinks my name is Mademoiselle.
He can whistle like the birds, and he has always
got time.

NICHOLAS BERTHOUD, with his chin on the top
of his stick: Those paintings, Mr. Galt, are finer
than Barraband's—the birds, just as they are,
on the wing, alive. I've seen him grow, since he
came here, and he's changed from painting dead
things in profile on the same old twig. Why, there
are as many as two hundred pictures in that portfolio on his shelf, and every one the bird to the
life!

MR. GALT (the botanist): Who is there to appreciate him here? He's a thousand miles from
Philadelphia, four thousand from men like Cuvier
and Swainson and Selby. He should go to Europe.

NICHOLAS BERTHOUD: I'm not so sure. They're a
stiff-necked crowd, museum men who like their
birds dead. In England he'd be an American and
a Frenchman, damnable both. In France—well,
there I'm prejudiced. But they're a closed circle
in Paris; before any one can get into the Académie,
somebody else has to die, you know. No, he's a
natural phenomenon, our friend, and there's no
place for him here or there. He's too late for Eden
and too early for the millennium. Perhaps he'll

not come back, one of these flights, and no one
will know where he was winged. Then you and I
will have to look out for that trump of a woman,
Lucy, and the babe.

It is the morning of the nineteenth of March,
1810, and a short figure half darkens the low door
of the business house of Rozier and Audubon.
From his account books, Audubon looked up, for
Rozier was busied with a woman buying print. The
new customer was a stranger, with burning eyes,
high cheek-bones and hooked nose—a narrow face,
alert, it seemed to Audubon, with a perpetual surprise—and he advanced, in his clothes so oddly
cut for the time and place, with two large volumes
under his arm.

Audubon gave him good day and asked him
what he might do for his service.

The stranger, like a Yankee trader, went to
the heart of his business without amenities.

"I am traveling," he said, putting down his
volumes on the counter, "to find subscribers for
my book upon American ornithology. Will you
allow me to show you these samples? I have here,
you see, the title page and some sheets of the letter-
press, and here are the illustrations which will ac-

company it. Lawson of Philadelphia has engraved them."

Audubon stared again into the odd countenance of his visitor, where it seemed to him that life's bitterness had overcast a very reserved and personal sweetness. "And may I ask your name, sir?"

"My name is Alexander Wilson. A poor man of whom you have never heard in these parts, but my betters have done me the honor to subscribe to my undertaking. Here is the list of them, sir. You see it contains names of preëminence in this country."

"It is not the men who have had the good sense to put their names down here that astonish me; it is the chance that I should happen here upon a man whose interests are so kindred to my own."

"Do you say so, sir? You are the first storekeeper I have found in that opinion. I have just come from Cincinnati, where a score of the wealthy and cultivated told me they would *think* about subscribing. They are a rare thoughtful people!"

His Scotch *r's* rolled out his bitter humor, and Audubon laughed with him.

"They don't know a hawk from a heronshaw in Cincinnati, I fancy. We are closer to the birds, down here."

"You're a hunter, I suppose."

"A tolerable good one. And now, Mr. Wilson," said Audubon, dipping his quill in the ink, "what is the price that you put upon your ornithology?"

"It is a hundred and twenty dollars, sir. And," he hastened to add defensively, for he saw the other's shock and hesitation, "it will be complete, sir, absolutely complete, the labor of many years and much hardship. And sold essentially at the cost of its publication, which I assure you is dear, very dear. I am seeking to do no more than to reimburse the engraver and the bookseller, who trust my honesty and the worth of my work."

Ferdinand Rozier had come up behind Audubon and was turning over the engravings curiously. There was silence for a moment, while the three men, each in his own way, were thinking about a hundred and twenty dollars. Alexander Wilson visualized that money as a bitterly poor man and a painfully honest one; behind him cracked the lash of his publisher; ahead of him stretched only years of humbled pride, begging from door to door, and the doors closed upon him. To Audubon money was a counter that you exchanged for the good and sweet things of life, and a man who had this book to sell need not have blushed to ask a thousand for it. Only, he hadn't a thousand to pay, and even a hundred and twenty spent on it was that much taken away from Lucy. And he had debts; people looked to him for honest return which they needed as much as he did. Yet here before him was science that he longed for. He fingered the quill unhappily.

Rozier, who knew best where the net balance really stood and took that view of a hundred and twenty dollars which is called realistic, knew also the weakness of his partner, not only his weakness for birds but that defect in his character on which he must now play.

"*Mon cher* Jean!" he complained, and went on in their native tongue, "Why subscribe to this work? Your drawings are certainly far better, and you know as much about the habits of American birds as ever this fellow does."

The little schoolmaster shot an angry glance at Rozier, and to Audubon said, "You are not so interested in birds, then, as you led me to think?"

"On the contrary," said Audubon politely. "Though I am no scientist like you, Mr. Wilson, it's my delight to draw them."

"Indeed! I had not expected to meet an artist

in Kentucky. Would you care to let me see any of your efforts?"

"Willingly, sir," said Audubon, and from under a bolt of cloth on the shelf behind him, he drew forth his portfolio, and turning it round on the counter for Wilson's inspection, he opened the vivid glories of his young art.

The astonishment on Wilson's face intensified, and Rozier, over Audubon's shoulder, grinned faintly at the discomfiture of this stranger. Whatever his partner was or wasn't, the good God knew he could draw birds—though only the good God knew what use there was in that. Beside Audubon's drawings, this peddler's were stiff and chilly.

Wilson turned over the sheets slowly, and said no word for some minutes. Then he spoke. "I had no idea," he said painfully, "that there was anybody else engaged in making such a collection."

"Our surprise is mutual," smiled Audubon.

Wilson's voice held a note of alarm. "You have the intention of publishing these?"

"Not the least in the world, my friend. I paint birds solely for my own delight."

Wilson rendered him a wintry smile. "You paint them beautifully. I wish that I had your talent; I was born nothing of an artist and have had to teach myself what little skill I have."

"I have never studied but by piece-meal, myself," said Audubon in a friendly way.

"Perhaps Nature does not endow a man with both art and science. Speaking as a scientist, I would like to ask you about several of the birds you have figured. Have you any specimens to authenticate them?"

"Indeed, Mr. Wilson, I have thousands—or rather, Nature has them in her keeping. I care nothing for a stuffed corpse, and when I've shot a bird I paint it at once, and at one sitting, for the brilliance of the plumage, I think, goes almost as quickly as the warmth of the little thing's body."

"I've seen him sitting at a drawing ten hours at a stretch," Rozier put in, with a kind of disgusted pride.

"Mm," agreed Wilson. "I should certainly like to have a look at the originals of some of these."

"If you are remaining in Louisville, Mr. Wilson, we can go out and hunt for them together, and I'll be glad to lend my drawings to such an eminent scholar as you are. Where are you staying?"

"I have taken a room at the Indian Queen tavern."

"I live there myself," cried Audubon. "It's near the dinner hour now—let us go back together, and I will present you to my wife."

This is the account of the famous meeting as Audubon gives it, and if I followed the quaint practice of Miss Mühlbach, who in her historical novels put in little asterisks to indicate that such were the queen's very words, I should be obliged to sprinkle more stars than usual over these pages.

The biographer is lucky when he has a second authentic perspective on his high moments, and in this case there is Wilson's own journal of his Louisville sojourn. It throws no light upon Audubon, who is mentioned only as a Mr. A., with whom he went out shooting. He remarks that even storekeepers live in taverns in Louisville, that he got not one subscription in that place, received no civility from any one there, and that science had not one friend in that community. He records examining Mr. A.'s drawings—"very good." But in his bird rambles, there was "no naturalist to keep me company."

What is the truth between these two testaments? Characteristically, one man practically obliterates the meeting, the other tells a flowing story in which he comes off gallantly. With equal gallantry, he confesses his mistake in not subscribing to Wilson's book; he owns his vanity, but alas! he does not stop there. In later years he was to charge Wilson with plagiarism from his drawings, a charge not in the least substantiated, so far as I can see, by a comparison of the moot plates.

All his happy life, the spectre of the short-lived Wilson haunted Audubon, and his many written references, most courteously doffing his hat to the little pioneer of American ornithology, never sufficed to still Wilson's partisan friends, crotchety Waterton, vindictive Ord. On both sides of the Atlantic, in the years to come, they plagued Audubon and sought by every means to prevent his publishing, to exclude him from learned societies, to charge him with theft, ingratitude, and false witness. Their task was made easier because Audubon was so plain a target; in Philadelphia as in London, he cut a queer figure, easy to ridicule and easier to envy.

Wilson was dead then. He could not hear the bickerings of those who took his name. The silence of the supreme dignity had enfolded him. His is a figure of pathos, and Audubon came to feel it. "Passed poor Wilson's schoolhouse," he once wrote in his journal, "and heaved a sigh . . ."

Even at their first meeting, Audubon had an impression of the tragedy in Wilson's life. The wanderer did not linger for easy talk after supper at the Indian Queen; he slipped away to his room, habitually secretive as a solitary sandpiper. And presently the Audubons, in their chamber, heard him solacing his heart with his flute. The air was old, some thin Caledonian lament. And John James, with Lucy in his arms, felt pity misting his own happiness.

A few days later, Wilson's room at the tavern was empty; they did not hear the flute again.

For us today that rivalry is dead. Wilson and Audubon have been honored as each deserves. True it is that Wilson the man has not been so well loved, but love is not just. To do him justice, you must yield to Wilson priority, a thoroughly scientific frame of mind, and courageous persistence. You have to remember that his boyhood had been darkened by slavery to the weaver's loom in Scotland; he had lived thinly and stonily, and in his breast a poet had died. When his *Wattie and Meg* appeared anonymously, all Scotland congratulated Bobbie Burns. When his satire touched the highly placed, he was compelled to burn his words in public. Thrice he was in love, and thrice rejected.

His teaching differed from his weaving only in that it was slavery of the head more than the hands.

In his adversity, as in Audubon's, only the birds were solace, and he journeyed, lonely, in ill health and poverty, through the forests and down the shadowy rivers, with only a little paroquet on his shoulder to bear him company. It was in Louisville, at the Indian Queen, that he parted with this little green companion, and, I think, with some less visible familiar that had sustained him. Alone in his unequal struggle with the western forest, on the river, in the rain and the night, he had been buoyed by pride in the work he thought unique. Now he had seen how greatly it was bettered. The rest of the way must have been harder for Alexander Wilson. It was not long. In three years more, dysentery and, they say, his publisher's dishonesty, had made an end of him. And there is now, in all the American forests, not one green paroquet left to remember him by.

XII

IN 1810 the Audubons and Rozier removed
from Louisville to Henderson, Kentucky, under
the hopeful impression that it was a thriving town
where business would be livelier. But as they came
around the bend of the river they saw that Henderson, like every other American community, had
advertised its intentions rather than its achievements. Here was only a group of log houses amid
the tropic-looking giant cane, our native bamboo.
Less than two hundred persons sheltered here, and
their needs were meagre and primitive.

John and Lucy made a home for themselves and
little Victor in a log-cabin. Its finest article of
furniture was their son's cradle, but he and Lucy
were too young, he remembers—lifting his hand
for a moment to let us see the hidden light beneath
it—too young and too newly married to be sad or
worried or at a loss for pleasures, and whatever
befell them, their young spirits and bodies were
resilient.

144

The American mind has never been ashamed of
the log-cabin and never too sorry for all those who,
though they did not become Lincolns, were born
in such. We go back and build them, for summer
homes, for camps and studios. And after that
dreamy villa by the Mediterranean, with its mirrors and servants and polished floors, my first
thought was of this little log room where the
plainness of things should not distract from the
spirit that is thought. There is no paint on the
wood, and the bark is left on the ash-tree beams,
and the bricks that make the hearth had lain a
long time in the weather, where an old home had
been burned, till they were rose and brown and
vaguely patterned. Only a threshold separates me
from real earth, and I step right out into asters
in the Fall and bird song in the spring.

So here I feel neighborly to John and Lucy
Audubon in their log-cabin in Henderson amid
the canebrake, and I can feel for them the distance
that lay between their hearth and her birthplace
at Burton-on-Trent—soft English rain falling
upon tender lawns, apple blow against a high garden wall of rosy brick, the smell of tea roses in
the air, the golden brown of books deep around
the walls. And he had La Gerbetière to remember,

and all of France, where a firm, harmonious and essentially moral civilization grows so naturally out of a culture that is agriculture. There the traveler without sense of change or shock passes through the granges and the stables, through the *jardin potagère*, to the orangery, the beds of gilliflower and sweet violet, through the box-maze to the doorway, and on to the salon with its fragile chandelier, its 'cello sheathed in velvet, its lovers in Sèvres, and thence, as his inclination guides him, to either of those two apartments that are *au fond de la vie*, the kitchen where an artist presides, the bedroom where goosefeathers will soften the sleep of one or a couple.

The charm of the Old World environment, for which we Americans annually pay millions, consists in a certain congestion—narrow streets, houses that lean upon each other, piece-meal fields, intimately limited by hedge and copse, so that wherever you go it is 'round the corner from everywhere else. The grand and charmless beauty of America is of a reverse order. I look out of the open door, and what I see, gazing west toward the prairie, is two unbroken miles of green grass carpet billowing over the subtle swell and fall of the glaciated terrain, and beyond it a border of woods following the river north and south, woods like hills or the sea, rising and falling with deep internal shadows of purple and blue and bronze. Between my cabin and those distant river woods there is just one other house. It is small and white and so far away that I cannot see the German-American gingerbread hanging from the eaves like the scallops on a valentine, but I can see three dazzling points of light on the lightning rods. Back of the house rises the great sustaining bulk of the barn, weathered to the color of a ripe Jonathan apple, and in the morning sunlight uprises the flanking geometrical beauty of the silo.

House, barn and silo—this is the *bloc*, the unit, the trinity that, repeated a thousand times but at generous distances, represents this countryside as the pine, the shoji and the curly hill make Japan for the artist, or the cactus, the sombrero and the white façade, Mexico. The public has begun to cheer now for this pattern of ours and its detail, but there are some who thought full twenty years ago that a silo was more beautiful in itself and in its meaning than the dungeon tower at Rouen where they tortured Jeanne d'Arc.

The beauty of America is distance, and there is no state in the union where you cannot get it.

Nothing calls you round the corner, but all the
continent calls you straight ahead and straight
ahead. That unheard music called young America
up; it made men who were comfortable rise slowly
with an ache in the bones and decamp, to begin
the hard way over again. Perhaps they thought
they were going west for money or another chance,
but if they thought at all they must have foreseen
more hardship than wealth. And it is a figure of
speech to talk about the westward course of empire. We have pushed out in all directions; there
is a lure about the north; the very word has a cold
ringing call; it sounds like an echo over a sheet of
water girdled by shadowy conifers and rocks.
There is a spell about the south, and if you have
ever seen palm hammocks rising over the everglades, you will remember them like an aching
dream, like a Don in armor who died before he
got to them and left his sword in the marsh. The
American is as willing to turn eastward now, and
I have heard a Californian speak wistfully of Ver-
mont. In truth, we do not know why we move, for
we are distracted with the beauty of our horizons.
America is all horizon.

The psychical meaning of the frontier is that
it was an horizon you could actually reach. But it

was seldom like the foot of the rainbow, and the Audubons and Rozier certainly found no pot of gold in Henderson. They sold little of their stock except pork, whisky, and powder, and when that was exhausted Rozier and Audubon took turns at a return trip to civilization for fresh purchases.

So it was that Ferdinand Rozier arrived one autumn afternoon at Henderson to find the store closed. No sign of Audubon or that squirrel-chasing young scamp of a clerk, John Pope. He saw a young girl turning away from the locked door and called to her to wait; he got out his own key, let her in, and noticed instantly how damp the store smelled and how dusty were the counters.

Rozier was tired and depressed, and nothing to-night awaited him except a lonely bed in a rough cabin, and he served his plain, thin young customer morosely. The girl reflected his mood, and though her purchases came to more than seven dollars, she seemed to lay the money down unwillingly, and Rozier was curt with his thanks. It was good to get seven dollars, but capital vanished by the seven hundred. The girl, with her arms full of bundles, went to the door and struggled for the handle. Outside, in the soft sunshine and high pig-

"Oh, I'll not be staying, thank you. I just came to find out what's become of Jean."

"He's out with the boy, to get game for all of us. The teal have been going over, and the bob-white are fat."

"No doubt," said Rozier dryly. "How long has he been gone?"

"I'm expecting him home any time," Lucy evaded.

"I asked you how long he had been gone, Madame."

"He shut up shop yesterday morning," said Lucy, "when the whole town turned out for pigeon. There's been none but women in the place ever since."

"Don't women ever buy anything?" asked Rozier sarcastically.

Lucy flushed. "Little enough when they know there will be pot pies for two weeks."

Rozier walked around the room with his hands in his pockets. "You set up a good defense, and not for the first time. But, Madame, why do you not look at the facts? Jean is off bird's-nesting, and we both know it. You aren't even sure whether he'll come home tonight or next week. And a bagful of birds or a basketful of perch isn't really what a

man keeps a family on. Far less a pack of drawings."

Lucy turned her back upon him, hiding her face
and her feelings, lest he should see how well he
had shot at the mark. She bent over the baby,
tucking in blankets, taking a long time about it.

"Well, Mr. Rozier," she said at last, straight-
ening, "you can't see what I see, and there are
dozens to agree with you about John. He isn't
made for business, and I wouldn't blame you if
you broke with him. Indeed, I can't see why you
don't. You're a clever man and you're industrious
and honest. Get free of John. And I'll wish you
every success. But together you'll never do each
other any good."

Rozier sank down on a bench. "You don't like
me, Madame Audubon. But I like you. You're a
fine woman, with lots of spirit, and better than
Jean deserves. I admire you, and I've got your
interest at heart. And all I'm saying is, look at
things. Look at this!" He waved his hand around
the meagre room.

Lucy looked, and smiled to herself. But that
Rozier did not notice.

"I've seen your father's home," he said. "I know
the old gentleman, and I knew Captain Audubon.

What if they could see the trail you have left—
their money gone, every step a step down?"

"That's how you measure things," said Lucy
evenly. "But half the people in the west have left
comfort and gentle living, and every step west they
call a step forward. And John—" She was silent,
and looked out of the dark window. "How can you
know where John is going?" she finished.

"Straight to ruin," he told her brutally. "I
can't influence him. I depended on you, Madame,
to make him feel his responsibility. But you don't
do it. It wouldn't be too late if you'd begin now.
I know you're in love with him, and it's natural
in love to give in. But see here—" and he smiled
at her, and nodded to the cradle—"there is the
little one. You must be a good mother."

Lucy's eyes darkened and she said nothing. He
got up and put a gentle hand on her shoulder.
"Take hold, Madame. Be an even stronger woman
than you are. You are very young, but young
women have a strength of their own. Jean is in
love with you too."

She looked at him, smiling, from some distance,
and removed his hand from her shoulder. "You
should get married, Ferdinand. There is much you
could learn."

"Well, I shall hope for Jean's good luck," he said, offering a truce to her, and taking up his hat. He played the last of his act astutely when he went to the cradle and picked up the fist of the child tenderly, and smiling at so much sleeping dependence, he shook his head and walked softly to the door.

Lucy watched him let himself out, and went methodically about getting the supper. She put two plates on the table. She built up the fire and got out the teapot and spoons and the loaf and the sugar. Her steps were light and certain.

Night over Kentucky. Many men coming home to many women. Many women alone, not knowing when their men will return, not certain that they will come at all. Men lonely by campfires and on barges, men without women, no longer able to put off the thought of them, white thoughts and red thoughts. Throughout the territory no other woman like this, no other with this straight, straight look, as she goes about in the shabby clothes that a bride was proud of once. But in all the world there is no pride like the pride of those who give all. If you cannot shake their faith, you can do nothing at all with them, though I do not say it is impossible to make them suffer. Debt is an ugly thing, and poverty is a harsh one, and laughter is a whiplash. It is a question now only of Lucy Audubon's faith. A woman may believe in a mistake. And in this hour there is no one to counsel Lucy, though there is small doubt what the counsel would have been. Lucy was a woman rich in sense, but it was uncommon sense.

The door was flung open, and John James stood in the frame of it, fresh autumn wind sweeping into the room and the autumn stars sparkling behind him.

"Lucy!" he cried, and she ran towards him, her finger on her lips, casting a glance at the cradle.

He shut the door, and now it was home.

"And so," he wound up his narrative at the table, "my Lucy will put her feet down in the mornings into Monsieur Cougar's hide, and we shall send a brace of ruffed grouse to the Rankins and a turkey to old Ferdinand when he gets home."

"He is home," said Lucy, cutting bread. "He got home this afternoon. He said the goods arrived safely from Shippingport."

"*Diable!* He caught me out again."

"We discussed that," Lucy said calmly. "There's no more to be said."

He looked at her as a boy may look at his

Barn Swallow.
HIRUNDO AMERICANA.
Male 1 Female. 2

Drawn from Nature by J.J. Audubon FRS. F.L.S.   Engraved, Printed & Coloured, by R.Havell 1834.

BARN   SWALLOW

mother whom he trusts to deal with matters above his head, and then reached over, smiling, and twined a tendril of her hair around his finger.

"Does thee not want to see my drawings that I have done?" he asked, promising her the best he had.

The dishes she only pushed out of the way, leaving them till later, to make space for the big sheets, and she stood in the crook of his arm and pored over them.

"Here is my owl," he said, "with the moon peeping out, do you see, behind him. And here is my kite, waiting on in grand style above a flight of pigeons. That's all I got done. But I saw so much!" And his eyes were full of it.

She felt already how far away he was from her, and it seemed as though she kept him almost better in the glory of his drawings than in his body beside her. But she knew she was not right in this; he had such need of her that she possessed him in all ways, and it was only this that she asked out of life. Call her blind, call her infatuate, call her reckless and seduced. But out of life she got that which she wanted, and in her turn she was loved as greatly and as warmly as she loved.

Above the cabin roof, in the deepening frost

and dark, the stars turned slowly on their glittering hub. The baby did not stir in the depth of his slumber. The fire tenderly lowered its light. Even in their great privacy the two voices sank to whispers, the two shadows sank upon the bed. There is an hour so complete in happiness, a man asks only that it be folded then in sleep.

XIII

"THE PLEASURES which I have felt in Henderson," runs Audubon's record, "and under the roof of that log cabin, can never be effaced from my heart until after death."

He was popular, he was affable, he was easy to get on with—all too easy to best in a bargain or hoodwink in a deal. For years after he left Henderson he was still the best topic for those southern tale-tellers who have to cap every story with a better one. They said he would follow a hawk three days, swimming rivers, wading through the cane-brake, till he could get a shot at it. That when divers were showing off their skill, he put them to shame by plunging from the bow of a vessel crowded with sight-seers, and only emerging at her stern. And that wife of his would strike out before any onlookers and breast the Ohio till she reached the Indiana shore. Those married couples that remain in love too long embarrass us. What shall we do with a man and wife who swim to an island on a workaday date and dig for turtle eggs like children playing castaways? Who merge with the deep greenery where the yellow-billed cuckoo calls in sultry solitude, as if they were half-gods, a centaur who has caught an echo in Kentucky's woods? Women wonder about a woman who keeps her girlhood through maternity; and in a man who takes his losses as though of little consequence, other men perceive a traitor to their constitution.

Detailed biographers record now a rapid shift in Audubon's partners. The last venture with Rozier was a remove to Ste. Geneviève in Missouri. Lucy and the babe were left at Dr. Rankin's hospitable hearth, and the two partners and the boy John Pope set off in their skiff in a December snow storm on their last ill-fated argosy. I will not describe what Audubon so vividly has in his journals, and what I have never seen—the ice jam where the Ohio and the Mississippi pile their blue floes upon each other into crackling mountains. Here with their wares piled in a disconsolate heap, their craft gripped fast in a tightening fist of ice, poor Rozier wrapped in his blankets slept the days away, moping like a moulting fowl. But John James was off with the eagles and the Osages and

Shawnees, and in that critical hour the practiced marksman was the more practical half of the partnership. They lived upon turkey breast buttered with bear's fat, and Rozier cursed and groaned and John James was contented as a winter duck.

Spring came; the two torrents broke upon each other with the sound of rival artillery, and the voyagers proceeded to their destination. The whisky sold to the French Canadian settlers at a profit of eight hundred percent, and Rozier was delighted. But the cautious iron-clad covenants of the partnership, drawn up by Audubon *père* and Rozier *père* so long ago, so far away, over wine, under a cool, reflective French sky, could bind these two beside the Mississippi no longer. They wrote each other out a mutual release, Rozier buying out Audubon's share of their cargo, and Audubon went back to Henderson, to Lucy and the store.

So much has been said about Audubon as a poor business man that it seems only fair to record that the store went better managed by Audubon alone. But times were hard in the west; the frontier continued to overleap itself commercially for the next seventy-five years. At this moment there was no possibility of selling to the east. The

Ohio Valley could only afford transport to New
Orleans by water, and export to Europe. And
Jefferson's one great political blunder, the Em-
bargo Act intended to spite England and France,
had simply cut off the American nose. What the
west lacked was capital, and to supply it, it was
mortgaged, to the haft of its ax, to the eastern
banks. Under these conditions, a community or
a country becomes a mass of lawsuits, wherein
men who cannot trade hope to find a legal way
of taking something from somebody else. There
was nobody who was showing a real net balance
of profit at that moment, and Audubon's affairs
would not have been too discreditably unsuccessful if he had not entered into partnership with
those who assured him that, as they understood
business, he must place his resources in their
hands. His warm friend and Lucy's brother
Thomas was the first to involve him, with an ambitious exporting firm, Audubon to be the buyer
of raw materials in Kentucky, he, Thomas, to be
the gentleman with offices in New Orleans which
would sell to the European client. But President
Madison, with a minute navy and no army except
the sons of Revolutionary heroes who supposed
they had only to remind the English of Yorktown

to win a war, had declared war on our best customer. Audubon was unaware how this had affected his fortunes, and was at Dr. Rankin's
house, engaged in drawing a river otter, when
Thomas arrived, moaning that all was lost, and
as abruptly departed, leaving his ruined friend
to finish up the otter.

Others now took Audubon aboard with them,
and their ideas were grandiose and fatal. There
was that mill, intended to grind wheat in a country that raised little, and to saw lumber in a
community of expert axmen. This gaunt and
dreary structure was erected at a cost of fifteen
thousand dollars, of which the other partners
jointly furnished less than half. A supposed expert installed the machinery that never worked
properly, and Audubon himself, so far from being
the gentleman investor relieved of active part,
gave sixteen hours a day of manual labor in
the dark and thundering interior.

When it failed, to a frightful total, a majority
of the investors seem to have taken the attitude
that Audubon was the Jonah aboard their vessel. Business really ought to have some sort of
an artist aboard every enterprise; he may prove
an immense convenience in cases of disaster. We

can imagine everything that Henderson said.
People are still saying it about Audubon, for
America is made up of Hendersons, though some
of them have a population of several millions.
People are still seeing through Audubon. A wonderful painter, and a charming fellow, but in the
affairs of life, you know, such as you and I excel
in, a child, a laughable dub. But just what are
"the affairs of life"? Each man's life is his own
individual affair, and Audubon's failure in the
mill was not one half so pathetic and complete
as your failure would be if you tried to draw
those petrels on my wall.

Perhaps I am a little harsh here, not with Audubon, but with the rest of us. Since 1929 it has
been discovered that the virtue of solvency is
frail. It is not maintained simply by the will to
pay your bills, nor even by endeavor, but by the
accident of being able to do so. Since many very
honest people, rich and poor, have suffered the
unforeseen accident of the depression, we have
had a great awakening to the comprehension that
there are many things in life worth trying for.
The only standard we still thoroughly trust is the
high American belief that trying will get you
there. By this criterion, Audubon is the most glit-

tering example of the virtuous success story in the national history.

But I am going to put myself on record as one who would still throw up his cap for John James, had he failed. Even if he had not hit the mark, I would admire no less what he was aiming at. People may smile indulgently for my sake when I say that the aims of the world are not innocent enough, they are not pure enough, they are not grand enough. Christopher Columbus was a conspicuous failure; Cortez was a conspicuous success. Jim Fisk and Dan Drew were notorious successes. But if Audubon had been a failure, he would have been no less the man he was. He would at least have wrecked no endeavors, parasitized no wealth, and he would have been true to his own profession. So much is open to any humble and honest man. But Audubon gave everything he had for the most beautiful thing he could see. He was devout before a face of deity. I do not mean only the birds he painted, I mean the face of life in its most smiling candor. And, devious ourselves, so few of us trust to that face. We so seldom recognize Nature as life. When some one, or luck, does us an ill turn, or when we are just but not kind to others, we say, "That's life."

But life is the hard, potent seed of a tree, life is the tilt of a buzzard's wing. Life is the womb; life is the out-reaching, knowledgeable tendril of the grapevine. Life is thrush song after rain, the rippling of a muscle under the seal's wet fur. It is anything living, but not the man-made troubles we call by that name. I only ask who it was in the brave America of 1812 who knew most about life, and best loved and served it?

I ought, I suppose, to go back and show every step that Audubon took towards his own business downfall, the steamboat he bought, the lots he acquired, the ninety-nine year leases that he took, the paper money he accepted, the law suits he got into, and his unsuccessful primitive lumbering operations. But some of them are only family traditions; others, recorded in Audubon's hand, are confused and only half comprehensible, and the rest we have on the testimony of his enemies. All I know is that in one way or another troubles tightened their coils around him, and the days grew darker and darker.

But the great rôle in this act is Lucy's. Three more children were born to her in these Henderson years, Rosa and Lucy and John. And in the midst of this sad epoch, while the lines were being

graven deeper in her lover's face and all the ignoble trials were harrying them both, tragedy
swift and irreparable came to the mother. Both
the little girls died.

There was one commodity which Lucy's neighbors gave her freely, and that was advice. We need
not guess what it was, but Lucy stuck to the
breach she was filling. The fight every day grew
grimmer, and disillusion came and sat down un-
invited in her house and watched her to and fro
all day. Not disillusion in her John; though
his mistakes were numerous enough, they were not
mistakes of draughtsmanship or love. But the
treachery of death, the subtlety of debts which
had brought no return and covered everything,
like mould in rainy weather, the sufferings of
child-birth and its slow stealing away of youth—
these were things she had not foreseen that day
in the phoebe's cave.

It was in 1819 that the grist mill finally failed.
The greatest of the loss fell to Audubon. And
the debts sown over the years rose up like iron
men and closed about him. The law's hand was
on his shoulder, and he went to jail for the sin
of insolvency. No course was open to him but a
declaration of bankruptcy, and his creditors de-

scended upon him like locusts. Everything he owned they took. That was little enough by now. Three items they left him, his gun and his clothes and that eternal portfolio of his—whose worth today, if the astute business gentlemen could have foreseen it, would rebuild the mill.

So they freed him and, plucked clean, a man whom few cared to know any longer, without a dollar in his pocket he turned his back upon the canebrakes and the straggling cabins of Henderson and set forth alone on foot to Louisville.

"This," he set down long after, when his pen would not tremble, "was the saddest of all my journies, the only time in my life when the wild turkeys that so often crossed my path, and the thousands of lesser birds that enlivened the woods and the prairies, all looked like enemies, and I turned my eyes from them, as if I could have wished that they never existed."

But there was a door for him to open at Shippingport just outside of Louisville, the door of Nicholas Berthoud. He was a Frenchman, descendant of noblemen, an old friend, and now the husband of Eliza, Lucy's little sister. He greeted Jean with a firm handclasp, clapped the

other hand around the drooping shoulders, and
led him in, calling to his wife to bring wine.

Audubon sank in a chair, shrugged his shoulders high, lifted his arms and let them fall again
like the pinions of an old bird.

"*Eh, mon vieux, c'est fini.* Now there is nothing
left. I am good for nothing. I have been a fool
and I have been cheated and I have been unlucky
too. My poor wife would have been better off if
she had never met me, and it would have been
better if the boys had never seen the light."

"Oh, now, *voyons,*" said Berthoud, playing
along for time till the wine came. "There can be
nothing left of you, certainly, after that long
walk."

"And now, *quoi faire, mon Dieu?* Do you know
any one, Nicholas, who wants a muleteer, a wood-
chopper, squirrel-barker, somebody to skin a pole
cat or paint a sign?"

"Well, now, maybe, maybe," said Nicholas
jovially. "Your talents, *mon ami,* are certainly
diversified."

"And worthless."

The wine came, dark red Medoc with some body
to it, and Eliza, putting down the tray, embraced
her brother-in-law with tenderness.

"And how is Lucy?" she asked compassionately.

"My dear child, your sister is a fortress and no trouble can take her. But there is not a smile left on her lips, unless she sees me look for it."

Berthoud interposed.

"You put me in mind of something just now, Jean Jacques. It's this sign-painting, as you might call it. You've tried to do everything except what you were born to do. You are an artist, *c'est tout*. Why not make the most of that?"

A light broke in Audubon's face. He remembered the time he had done the portrait of an Osage chieftain, that glorious and catastrophic winter when he and Rozier were ice-bound at Cash Creek, and he recalled too that his own delight in the likeness had almost equalled that of the brother in war paint.

"*Tiens!*" he cried. "That's an idea you have! If only I had taken off the likeness of Daniel Boone when I went squirrel-hunting with him! But now I shall do all the belles in calico and sell the portraits for five dollars apiece to their sweethearts!"

"And the children, John," suggested the delighted Eliza. "Every mother wants a picture of her child."

"Wait a minute," Nicholas broke in, "we must get you in demand, first. Now here's my suggestion: draw your first pictures for nothing, and draw them in the street when you can. These crowds love to gawk. Half of them haven't even got mirrors, and pretty soon they'll be paying handsomely just to have their own faces to look at all day."

And they did pay, and more money entered John's pocket for the work of an hour than for a day's slavery in the mill. People crowded to him, and he began to save money to send for Lucy and the children. It was only a precarious perch that he could foresee, but it was at least a home builded in his own element. He was called to do a child in her new dress, an old woman holding her Bible, a tall boy in his coffin. A minister had his newly dead little girl lifted from her grave that Audubon might catch something of those fleeting features. So starved humanity was, then and there, for the precious mortal personality that, cheaply and instantaneously, the photograph will now capture for you.

I see him alone, one night, with a dying man; they had come twenty miles to fetch him and his crayons to the big lonely house on the bare hill.

The doctor had gone, because his duty now was with those he could save, and Audubon had sent the family away to rest, telling them that he would call them if he saw a change. He worked very swiftly over the features of this stranger who was his brother man and of whom he knew nothing. But the face was there, and all that life had done to it, and something, he suspected, ancestral came out in it, the traces of the men and women who had made this man without dreaming upon him. And he saw that it was a great privilege to draw a human face, and to draw it free of all posturing, to give it exactly in its quiet, unlying personality. The face need not be beautiful; it suffices that it is itself, as it is enough that the hickory bark is shaggy and the suit of the little juncos a sober gray and black like the winter woods and the winter sky. To paint a man or a bird or a tree simply as it is, to live your life with a great love for life, to leave sons behind you, to leave something done as well as you could do it, to have loved a woman with honor and with fire, these would suffice a man, yes, these would suffice him.

Swiftly the pencil whispered across the page; his eyes moved quickly between the two like faces, and suddenly, looking more closely to verify a shadow, a curious change of planes, John saw that this pioneer on the bed had crossed the invisible frontier.

He put the pencil down, laid his drawing aside, but he did not instantly call the others. He went to the window, the sense of mortality closing his nostrils, and opened it. From the bottom of the night, from the woods below this hill, welled up a random, unawaited bird voice, one note so repeated, so emphasized, so inflected with a pensive assertion of life, that the listener took heart for all the years to come. With the silence of death behind him, with failure and disgrace just past, he was free once more in his wilderness, for the moment that the vesper sparrow sang.

XIV

"YOU THERE, Jo Seeg? You and your grog bottle? Or is that just the bottle over there in the shadders?"

"I'm here, Loveless. Is that you, or you and a woman?"

"No such luck as a woman on this flatboat. Think it'll take us a year to reach New Orleens? Think we're in the Mississip' yet?"

"Blacker'n sin outside. I can't tell. Hey, Cap'n Cummings, is this still the O-hi-o?"

"You'll have to ask Captain Aumach; he's the skipper," said the army man from his dark corner. "My trust's in him and the Lord."

"He's durned timid of the stream," criticized Loveless.

"How would you like to go aground?" asked Captain Cummings. "And have to fetch out in this frosty weather and go in up to your neck to push her off?"

"Gawd, it's lonesome," said Loveless. "Nothing

but islands and river and those big, solemn-looking cypresses and all that worthless big cane, and a lot o' snags and sawyers that'll snatch the pants off your boat in a minute."

"Off your boat, maybe," put in Jo Seeg, "but not Cap'n Aumach's. Have a nip and you'll feel better."

"I say it's lonesome," mourned Loveless. "It's a dead lot o' galoots we got aboard. Them two carpenter boys from Philadelphia, solemn as owls. And that kid John Mason, only eighteen and don't know no more about life than if he was a baby."

"Don't know all you do about wimmin," said Jo Seeg. "But he's a good kid and strikes me better'n that teetotallin' Audubon in there. Thank Gawd he takes snuff, anyway."

Captain Cummings arose and went to the door and stepped into the next cabin.

" 'Pears he don't like our talk," said Seeg, nettled.

"He's on good terms with Audubon."

"What's the teetotaller doin' in there now? Still got a candle goin', I see."

"Drawin' them birds of his again. Calls it 'sketchin'.'"

"What kind of birds is it this time?"

"How'd I know? Real *little* birds. Damnedest littlest birds in the country. Them he calls 'wobblers.'"

"He drew wobblers last week," Seeg complained.

"My Gawd, how ign'ant you are. They's fifty kinds of every kind of bird, didn't you know that?"

"Yeah, but listen. Sometimes he's good. Remember that eagle he done, eatin' a big catfish with its ol' head tore off? I'd 'a' been proud to have that. Dropped the bird on the wing plumb half across the river, and then look at the way he fixed it up with a lot o' little wires, just as nacherel as life, and then went to work and drawed it for six hours without a stop, till you could see every little feather. I watched him. That was a real day's work, that was."

"Day's work!" snorted Loveless. "Where'll that ever get him?"

"I dunno," admitted Seeg. "Seems like there was more sense in drawin' pictures of people that can pay for them."

"Fi' dollars a head, he gets. Ain't no bird goin' to pay fi' dollars. But I'd 'a' give twenty-five for that lady he sketched at Paducah. Got those eyes beautiful, and all that curly hair, and a mouth like it was askin' you to kiss it, and dress cut way down just where—"

"Go wash your mind and hang it up to dry," said Seeg, with a sound of rolling over.

The other was silent, and lay with torrid thoughts of what he would draw if he had the trick of it.

In the next cabin the boy John Mason and the dog Dash were already asleep. Cummings pulled on his pipe, as he tilted back in his chair, his feet cocked on the table.

"You don't mind me here, Mr. Audubon?" he wanted to know.

The crayon lisped across the page in many short, sure strokes, before the artist answered.

"If I minded anything it wouldn't be you, my friend. But I've no time for temperament. I can't insist on a north light, and that sort of thing."

"Gainsborough wouldn't have called these two candles any light at all. Why don't you wait till morning?"

"Because by daybreak anything may be coming overhead. Or we may make Cairo, if we haven't passed it, and I'll want to go ashore and bag what I can. I've sworn to paint a hundred birds on this voyage."

The Captain regarded him curiously as he worked. "Do you mean to make a livelihood out of this, Mr. Audubon?"

"When the good God pleases."

Cummings grunted skeptically.

"In the meantime—" He broke off, and worked swiftly over an alteration of line, his eyes flitting back and forth from the page to the little wired birds on the table. "In the meantime, I can support myself with portraits."

"Yes, you can support yourself," said the Captain, blowing out a jet of violent smoke.

Audubon laid down his pencils and looked the other man in the face. "You are thinking that my wife is supporting herself and my children, teaching school in Cincinnati. I know what they said about me there. Some said that no American would live on his wife, and some said she'd best be free of me. But I have listened too long to what other people say. I will tell you—I have made many mistakes in my life, but the one great mistake was listening to other people."

"What does your wife say?" inquired Cummings wonderingly.

Audubon smiled, and took up his pencil again. He gave the Captain a bantering paraphrase of the truth. "She said I must be a genius, since I certainly wasn't anything else."

For a while, just recently, he had tried to be a taxidermist. The position offered him in Cincinnati's infant museum of natural history had a regular salary attached to it, and John James had worked so zealously to earn it that he had very nearly labored himself out of a job. But if there had been enough material for a taxidermist's lifetime there, Audubon would not have stayed. A dawn of conviction was clearing his mind and lightening his heart. One by one the birds were taking up their chorus; it was swelling to a call he could not deny. Horizons beckoned him on, and he knew that he had to go to them. He would still have to do the hardest thing in the hardest way, but it would be his own way now.

And by his side Lucy was risen, seeing what he saw, believing with perfect confidence now in her husband's destiny, and taking from his hands the support of herself and their children. So there she was now, keeping school back in Cincinnati, to the scandal of the neighbors, having turned her odd husband loose to the birds. Now she was a schoolma'am. For all the world like a widow or a spinster, ringing the bell, giving out lessons, guiding handwriting, correcting ciphering, day in, day out, and that man of hers off on Jacob Aumach's flatboat with his dog Dash and a crew of riffraff, bound for who knew where?

The last of his old unhappy life had dropped away from him like jetsam on the river bank, as he drifted slowly past Henderson "about sunrise. I looked on the mill perhaps for the last time, and with thoughts that made my blood almost run cold bade it an eternal farewell." There it stood, bleak and angular in the rosy light, still mossed over with debts. There lay Henderson, friends and foes yet asleep. Somewhere in the dew-wet ground lay his little daughters, but sorrow itself was dead now, and the sun was rising. He did not look long at the town; he faced forward, his shoulders light, freed of that peculiar dishonor suffered by those who live lives for which they were never intended.

So he sailed into the morning of his adventure. All the birds of America were bound south upon their great autumnal flight, the plovers and the loons and ducks first to escape the oncoming arctic winter, the ibises and herons and whooping cranes lingering still in the balm of the days and the warmth of the brown waters. Now all that tropic

crew, orioles, tanagers and chats, were on the wing,
but many birds still called as if asking them why
they went, those fleeting insect-eaters, those bright
of wing and brave only in fair weather. At times,
as if fear had suddenly overtaken them, there
would band together for courage a flight of swifts
or nighthawks or a long preposterous defile of
pelicans. They passed John Audubon with a rush
of wings in the night; they trailed against the
yellow sinking moon. And by day the little warblers blew like a scattered shower through the
falling leaves in the woods, and after them, picking up the crumbs of the year, came the first little
snowbirds and juncos like flakes from the clouds
in the north.

The flatboat reached the Mississippi, and turning due south now, Audubon had his back to winter. He was going, as the birds went, with the
light, to the warmth. Life dealing with him more
gently every day. Pines on the hills, the river
looping in great oxbow bends. Blue-green islands,
festooned with lianas. The first magnolias with
their scarlet fruits above a glittering evergreen
breadth of leaf; November roses around old
houses with deep verandas and thin columns
double-storied in height. Wine-red bayous lost to

some stagnant enchantment of their own, black faces, easy voices, big water-melon laughter. At Natchez, holes in his boots, and a cobbler who would shoe him for a portrait. Fresh game for the boat's whole company, and so, at the river's lazy gait, Louisiana at last, the French language, live-oaks and Spanish moss and birds that he had never seen before.

For Louisiana even in winter is as blessed with birds as many a northern land in summer; it is the permanent home of so many creatures of the air who know no reason that they should ever leave it; it is the winter solace of so many others. Its bird life has a strong tinge of the tropic. Audubon saw black vultures walking in the streets, as in any Mexican village; the chuck-will's-widow called in the woods; ground doves were feeding on the rice standing in its pale flooded fields. On the bayous the pelicans yawned monstrously, and the snowy egrets thrust snaky necks among the water weeds.

Sheet by sheet, the bird drawings were filling the portfolio. When there should be enough of them, and every one of them satisfied him, he would try, he had determined, to publish them. This was now the single aim and hope of his existence.

It was well that he had no conception of the difficulties, the costs, and the rebuffs in his path. He had no idea of the politics of publishing, or those of art and of science. That his ambition was absurd there were many people to tell him. But he believed in himself now and Lucy believed in him. All his life he had been helped, and generously helped, by her people and his own, to be something that he was not. And he had lost all that had been given him. He was flung stripped upon his own resources. He was left alone with himself to look at the quality of man he was. A dreamer? Yes, a dreamer who had come awake to find that the dream was true. From this point on—and we have the journals he now kept, to prove it—there is no wavering in the man; no one can shake him.

Determination is a fine thing, but why should a man draw birds? Governor Tompkins of New York had voiced a wide-spread indifference when he told Alexander Wilson that so far from subscribing a hundred and twenty dollars for a book about birds, he wouldn't give that much for the whole flock of 'em alive. We are still most of us Tompkinses. In books or alive, the birds are less than a luxury to us. They are one of the many things we look at and do not see. For any man the thought of losing his eyesight is a horror, but at what a miserable lot of sights are we content to gaze!

That is why we need the artists. They see what we ought to see and show it to us. They cry aloud the beauty of the world, sunlight in a Vermeer, shadow in a Rembrandt.

I know that Audubon did not paint birds as most artists would. Pure art can only use the essence of an object; it will give you its emanation through an impression. And in the few birds that I can remember in the great Italian and Dutch masters there is little more to be gathered than the sense of flight. The Japanese will make a bird the center of their composition, but the composition is the thing.

I have said that the reality of Nature is not esthetic. And the paintings of Audubon are not esthetic. They are Nature. That this is just what he intended is seen in his determination to draw every bird to life size, from tit to eagle. His drawings are science almost unconsciously in their fidelity to what he saw, and he saw everything, how every feather lay and how the light lay on every feather. There could be, there are, better scientific drawings of birds, but science is only the order that man makes out of Nature for his own satisfaction. It is not greater than Nature, and neither is art. To me art and science are the dearest pursuits of life, but note that they are both in pursuit of Nature. And Audubon, who was an imperfect artist and scientist, is one of the few men who have ever caught her.

Arrived in New Orleans, though he was penniless, Audubon went in search of a copy of that work to which unfortunately he had not subscribed—Wilson's *American Ornithology*. For he was beginning to need a link now with kindred spirits. There had been birds, gulls and gallinules, warblers, snipes and sparrows, that he knew intuitively were strange and more than likely undescribed in science. Wilson had passed this way before him; what had he found, what passed unmarked? The *Ornithology* showed to Audubon that in his swelling portfolio he had captured birds new to science. And a new excitement ran in him. In the artist the scientist stirred and stiffened. He was finding his balance, finding his wings, the equipoise of a hawk, a hawk's-eye view.

The most honest vanity, and the one a man can safest show, is in accomplishment laid at the feet of the woman who loves him. I like to think of the glow in this man as he tied up the sixty drawings that he sent to Lucy from New Orleans.

There is no record of how she received them. But women's struggles are monotonous, and all days for Lucy must have been workadays. She was lonely; she was living on hope; her clothes were old, her children were little; strangers surrounded her. To feel what she felt when John's drawings came, you have to open the great sixty-pound elephant folios of *The Birds of America* for yourself and for the first time.

Suddenly the world is filled with wings. It is as if the grouse began to drum, the woodpeckers to drill, the wild geese to call to each other and all the warblers to burst into tiny song among flowers and leaves. A master hand is here whose strokes are free, whose color is real. Nothing is sweetened; the bill, the claw, are there, the grace in awkwardness, and into the spirit of each bird Audubon throws himself with abandon. Some love him for his jeweled hummingbirds in a tangle of blossoms, some for his falcons and great staring owls that fill a page large as the table where I work. But whatever emotion you have about these pictures, it is not the emotion of the artist. The birds are in no way humanized or cut to fit a design. Nothing but bird emotion comes out of those glowing plates. There are the bloody lust of the hawk, the gluttony of the grackles, the wind-tossed, wave-beaten courage of the petrels, the sweet watery contentment in song of the marsh wrens about their nest, the quarreling of the woodpeckers, the love of the two barnswallows for one another as they sit close together on their nest under an old beam.

I see Lucy lay down the last sheet and tie them all together again precisely. I see her walk to the window and look out on a winter world, Cincinnati in one of its yellow mists. Her back is very straight and she presses her fingers on the pane until they hurt.

She has no way to take the world and shake it. Every drawing cries out life and the glory of life, but who is there to listen? A thousand miles away John is alone, unrecognized, and here, each night, his wife is without his arms. There are Victor and little John to watch over; she must patch up their bruises and cure their sore throats. There are childish intelligences and wills to be captured and trained, parents to satisfy, neighbors to face, and all the mouse-holes to watch where a penny may slip down.

But Lucy was sure now, I dare to think, that the birds would set them free. She swept up the drawings in her arm with a laugh of pride, as if they were a darling child, and bore them triumphantly up the dark stairs, to her room where there would be only happiness tonight under her pillow.

XV

LIKE A portrait by a country photographer, with every wrinkle smoothed out and the head in a brace, are the early biographies of Audubon. The remark applies to Audubon's own accounts of himself as he posed them for the world. Just as he had long ago touched up the story of his birth, so he quite humanly made himself the hero of every encounter and put an order and sequence into events which are not found in life.

I found it startling to pick up his only very recently published journals that he began to keep on that Mississippi voyage. Here was not only the unvarnished truth—and it is sometimes quite painful reading—but the man himself, a hundred times more lovable and comprehensible for all the little wrinkles and the grain of the flesh. You may know the main events of a man's life and base an opinion of him on them, but acquaintance with a thousand trivial details of his living will certainly work upon that opinion. If it is not changed, it will be intensified. And so Audubon's daily thoughts, still fresh as the ink was wet that he wrote them down in, make him twice Audubon for me.

And he provides me with everything I could ask. In those Mississippi jottings I found Jo Seeg and his bottle, Mr. Loveless and his hankerings after the women-folk, Dash, and her whelps littered on the twentieth of December, and those two little warblers sketched by candle-light. I can tell you what Audubon thought of the French Creoles of Louisiana, whose portraits he painted and at what prices, and every bird he noted on every day. I know in just what mood he woke up in New Orleans on the thirteenth of January, 1821. "I rose up early, tormented by many disagreeable thoughts, again nearly without a cent, in a bustling city where no one cares a fig for a man in my situation."

Now on this same day I am going to precede Audubon to the warehouse of Mr. Pamar, down on the wharves, and wait for him there. Mr. Pamar is not aware that Audubon is on his way; he does not know that figure coming down the dock between the trundled barrels and the cotton bales. The lean black slaves straighten to look at him, with his long hair flowing and his deep-set eyes, and call incomprehensible gumbo comments to one another, as dogs bark of a stranger who does not smell of the caste.

Mr. Pamar in private life was a doting father, a faithful husband, and a generous host to his friends. But in his warehouse he was surrounded by slaves and beset by that type of well-spoken ne'er-do-weel in which New Orleans was just then particularly rich. Mr. Pamar was not a snob. He judged men not by rank but what they were good for. A man was as good as his word, a man was good for fifty thousand dollars. Or he wasn't. Included among those he called ne'er-do-weels were some of the colonial French families of New Orleans. The original Creole population—a middle-class aristocracy with a few nobles—was already in decay at this date, and in its place there was rising the great cotton plutocracy that forms so much of what we now remember, from the distance of the years, as "the old aristocracy of the South."

There fell a knock upon the door. Mr. Pamar barked "Come in!" and bent farther forward over his desk. Audubon came in with his light French tread, his woodman's quiet. Mr. Pamar, not detecting the soft closing of the door, glanced around. Fellow with a portfolio. Out to sell. He buried himself in his papers defensively.

With his hat in his hand like a cavalier and his locks tossed back, Audubon came alongside the desk and took a light stand there, smiling.

"Good day, sir," he said.

Mr. Pamar did not answer. He appeared to be very busy with figures and orders, but he was not really concentrating. He was aware of a fresh, disturbing presence—something like a draught, he thought irritably. Well, let the fellow out with it, whatever it was he wanted.

Audubon stood waiting for an answer to his greeting. It was cold and lonely where he stood, outside Mr. Pamar's recognition, and he answered himself with inner mockery. "Probably not a good day at all, John." Still he waited, courteously.

Mr. Pamar, exasperated, realized that he must be a gentleman.

"Good day," he said. "You have business to do with me?"

"Possibly," said Audubon, putting out a pawn.

"Will you state its nature?"

"I am a portraitist."

Mr. Pamar instantly thought of the children he doted on. Family portraits were the next thing he owed himself. A rich effect at a moderate price. He smiled; he was really a genial man at heart.

"Well, Mr.—?"

"Audubon."

"Mr. Audubon. You have done portraits in this city?"

"No one in this city. I have just arrived from Kentucky. May I show you some of my work?"

Mr. Pamar's eye traveled without interest over some drawings of orioles and redstarts, but he was arrested by a white-headed eagle in life size. Now an eagle was something to draw!

"Have you seen Vanderlyn's paintings?" he conversed. "He's got most of the trade in town. And a mighty fine painter. He's at work on a panorama of this city right now that's going to be the biggest painting in New Orleans."

The peddler-painter's deep-set eyes twinkled and his fine mouth was grave. "I must see that," he murmured. He quietly laid the lightly sketched head of a little girl before the other, a drawing all modesty and grace.

It touched Mr. Pamar's weak spot. He could see his own little beauties on paper, putting all the other drawings out.

"Well, Mr. Audubon," he said cautiously, "possibly I might find something for you to do."

The frosty pride that had held up Audubon so far in his unhappy entry into New Orleans thawed treacherously.

"I should be unspeakably grateful, sir," he said eagerly. "My needs are great. I have a family. I am not known."

Mr. Pamar looked up, and looked him over quickly with a business eye. "Just so, just so," he murmured. He saw now the shabbiness of the fellow, that his cavalier air had cloaked. He perceived that Audubon was no success, and if he was not, it followed logically for Mr. Pamar that he was not good for much. It is the Mr. Pamars of this world who sometimes make it so difficult for an artist to rise.

"Well, I'll tell you how it is, Mr. Audubon. If I were going to have any portraits made in my family, I would go right around to Mr. Vanderlyn. But cotton is very low this year. The Liverpool prices"—and he picked up a sheaf of papers and let them drop again—"wouldn't pay a nigger's wage. So you see," he said, guiding Audubon by a gesture to the door, "it's out of the question."

Audubon stood in the doorway with his hat in

his hand and the dry laughter of disappointment in his eyes. He made his dancer's bow.

"Good day, Mr. Pamar."

"Good day, Mr. Audubon," said Mr. Pamar, bowing, and he shut the door.

Of that meeting Audubon wrote just one line in his journal. It is this: *Audubon was poor today, and Mr. Pamar knew it, when he made his bow.*

But Nicholas Berthoud, who was by good fortune in New Orleans at the time, knew his Pamars, if he did not know portraiture, and the next day he made his brother-in-law retrace his steps to the warehouse on the wharves, propelling him by a friendly hand clapped on his shoulder; by the other hand he led his little girl. When the negro dockhands did not see Berthoud in time to get out of his way, he gave them a prod, on thigh or buttock, with the tip of his walking-stick, and they leapt from it as if it had been a water-moccasin. They saw their strange character of yesterday in lordly company, and wondered now if they had mocked an Elijah.

Berthoud knocked at the office door and went in without waiting for an answer, greeting Mr. Pamar with a well-measured cordiality.

"I want you to know my brother-in-law," he

began, intentionally ignoring that unfortunate meeting of yesterday. "Mr. John James Audubon, the finest portraitist from up in our country, but a man so modest that he goes around with letters of introduction from Henry Clay in his pocket, and presents himself as if he were an old peddler."

"My dear Mr. Audubon," said Mr. Pamar genially, "I don't care what Henry Clay thinks of you, but if my friend Mr. Berthoud here speaks well of you, that's enough for me. You ought just to have mentioned his name to me,"—Mr. Pamar was stretching a point, but he was sincerely eager to correct any errors in his own judgment—"and we could have come to a rapid understanding."

"Poor old Audubon," laughed his relative, gilding him with an admiring glance, "probably represented himself as absolutely flat. When he thinks what he's doing, he's one of the most prosperous men in his profession. But, you see, just before he came to see you, he'd been out to the fête, helping you all celebrate the anniversary of General Jackson's victory over the British, and he let somebody pick his pocket. He may be a genius, but, about these things, he's a terrible greenhorn."

Audubon's face lighted up puckishly. "I don't

know about the color of my horns, but those of some of these Creoles ... !"

Mr. Pamar threw back his head and laughed. "Let's have a drink on that. ... I don't know how you gentlemen will think this compares to your Kentucky whisky, but here's your health! ... So, you've formed your opinion of these compatriots of yours, Mr. Audubon?"

"It's a sorry lot of relatives to have to own," said Audubon. "They speak neither good French, good Spanish, nor good English, and if the temperature drops a point below summer heat, the gentlemen turn their collars up and hold their handkerchief in front of their noses. What would they do on the Rocky Mountains?"

"And the Creole ladies, how do you find them, Mr. Audubon?"

"Not to my taste, sir. I don't care for these sallow cheeks. I like Yankee roses better." And he pinched the little girl's cheek.

"I should like mighty well to have you do some pictures of my family, Mr. Audubon. It's just a question of whether I could touch your price."

Mr. Pamar was secretly amazed, upon hearing that only twenty-five dollars was the fee; yesterday he would have been surprised that it was as much as that. He did not really wish to drive a bargain, but his habits were ingrained.

"Well, we could put all of my four children on one picture," he suggested to the bottom of his whisky glass.

Berthoud shot John a warning glance, and Audubon replied with golden sweetness. "That is perfectly feasible—for one hundred dollars."

Decidedly, Pamar thought, he had miscalculated this man's talents. He rubbed his chin with his thumb. "The matter, after all," he parried, "lies with Mrs. Pamar. You know how mothers are about their children. And she hasn't seen your work, as I have."

"A pity you didn't bring your portfolio, Jean," put in Berthoud. "You might have sent it round to her. But, here! Here's a little model for you." And he fingered a lock of the child's hair affectionately. "Take off a sketch of her and we'll dispatch it to Mrs. Pamar and wait for her verdict."

Audubon agreed with a smile, but the smile was over his brother-in-law, son of a French marquis, who so thoroughly understood American business methods and the art of salesmanship. Even Berthoud, he knew, thought his ornithological projects the illusion and mania of a madman. But whatever his private opinion of his wife's sister's husband, Berthoud came forward with staunch family good will to set his odd relative forth in the best possible light.

Audubon knew that it was no time for raising difficulties that might seem temperamental. He accepted a commercial pencil and a large sheet of wrapping paper. Mr. Pamar admired large pictures; Berthoud evidently conceived that there was no reason why a portrait should not be made in a quarter of an hour, in any sort of light; and the little girl, set up on an accountant's stool, reached into her dress to find her locket and set it primly on her breast. The stage was set and he was expected to perform to the satisfaction of the unknown Mrs. Pamar.

An hour later a negro returned with a favorable response and Berthoud had nailed his poor old Jean an order for her portrait as well as the children's.

Now this is a pleasant sequel to find in the journal, to that one bitter line of the day before, but how many thoughts about it Audubon must have had that he did not set down! He must have thought that it is a wry world in which you must pretend not to need the money you want to earn;

not all the world is thus; this is a provincialism of our own. He must have thought that it was kind of Nicholas to manage this affair so much better than he had, and have tasted the gall of that obligation. He must have passed an amused and shrewd judgment upon the too shrewd Mr. Pamar —who afterwards became his very warm and generous friend. And he must have felt, like a cold void about him, the lack of understanding, in these excellent men, of his aims.

He was facing now, without wishing to be a portraitist at all, the humiliation of the unknown portrait painter who has not the standing of a pure artist among artists nor that of a man of the world among the worldly people he must paint. Without any wish to teach drawing, he was obliged to become a drawing teacher. Lessons in art in those days were taken largely by young ladies of wealth who would have shuddered away from the idea that they might ever become artists. And Audubon summed up his experience of such pupils with these words: "When you are employed as a teacher to any ostentatious or opulent person— *flatter*, keep flattering, and end in flattery, or else expect no pay."

To the artist it is always a confusing thing that

a very mediocre talent in commerce commands a salary on which one may live at a certain scale, while his own talent, which people profess to admire as so mysterious and enviable, is a waif that must go from door to door. In time, of course, it may find that every door flies open, but between the old days of the ducal patrons and the possible future when the State shall nurture the young artist, there seems no place for him to lay his head.

His struggles are rendered more baffling, at times, by fellow craftsmen who have carved out some special success. The epitome of Vanderlyn's was "Marius in the Ruins of Carthage." Also, he built an exhibition hall called the Rotunda, then considered immense, in City Hall Park, New York, expressly designed to show his immense panoramas. At the moment when Audubon found himself in New Orleans, Vanderlyn's style of painting was already a mania with the public, which was prone to compare all art by those Carthaginian standards. The door to success seemed to be Vanderlyn's door, and thither John James took his way, the now dog-eared portfolio under his arm.

He was kept waiting for some time in the spacious hallway, while guests and sitters came and went in the drawing-room of which the backwoods-man caught glimpses when the negro butler opened the double doors. Finally a message came out that if Mr. Audubon would be pleased to leave his portfolio, the busy artist would presently look it over. Audubon laid his portfolio upon the marble-topped console and remained seated, not far from it, waiting with a now grim patience.

Fashionable New Orleans, still affecting the velvet *culotte*, the buckled shoon and periwig of an extinct France long lost to them, tripped by, flicking a glance of astonishment or amusement at the figure in the nankeen coat, with the deep, prophetic eyes. At last Vanderlyn, emerging from his salon in the company of an elegant captain of artillery, caught sight of him too.

"Ah! Oh, yes, of course; this is Mr.—ah?"

"Audubon," said John, rising.

"Audubon. Yes.... Well, Mr. Audubon, you wished to show me some of your efforts?"

"I have left them, as you sent word to me to do, on the table."

Vanderlyn flushed slightly, and begging the captain to excuse him a moment, tossed back the cover of the portfolio like an uninterested man in a hurry. Then the tempo of his gestures changed.

He picked up one sheet after another slowly and studied them.

In the pause, which the mandolin clock on the wall counted out, the dapper captain strolled up to his friend and looked over his shoulder.

"Gad!" he said, bending sharply to see better. "Look at that wild turkey, Vanderlyn. Why, it's alive!" He turned cordially. "You could sell that, sir; these Creoles are passionate sportsmen—kill thousands of golden plovers a day. That would make a damn fine dining-room piece, that would."

"Yes, very good, very good." Vanderlyn spoke kindly, from a height. "Where did you learn to draw, Mr. Audubon?"

"I'm self-taught, sir. Excepting some instruction from David in Paris, in my youth."

"Well," cried Vanderlyn, descending a bit, "we have that in common! I was at the Louvre with him."

Like the good Mr. Pamar, Vanderlyn, now that he knew where to place this man and where it was safe to rate him, could deal more confidently with him. In the end he graciously wrote out a recommendation in which he asserted that he had seen the drawings of Mr. Audubon and considered that, as a painter of birds, he was "excellent."

Tucking it quietly into his pocket, Audubon descended the broad white steps at Vanderlyn's house with the ring of irony still binding his heart. Vanderlyn had regarded, even jealously, the draughtsmanship; he had not seen the birds—the wild province that Audubon was making his own. But a word from those in power, even an oblique one, even a statement that misunderstands your purposes, even a cool and grudging approbation, will carry the unknown so far that whatever scorn they feel for it must be mixed with their gratitude.

Audubon turned down the street, and at first paid no attention to the sound of hurrying footsteps behind him. His arm was caught from behind, and he half turned, to meet the flushed and earnest face of the artillery officer.

"I just wanted to tell you, Mr. Audubon," he said breathlessly, "that Vanderlyn thinks you're tremendous. Oh, he doesn't know a bird from a bat, but he knows a good drawing when he sees it. He'd have shown his feelings if his nose weren't so out of joint. Pity he didn't. I wanted you to know."

Audubon's brown eyes shone on him with a

gentle light. "And you ran after me to tell me that?"

"Yes. No, dash it, I wanted to tell you how good *I* thought they were. I'm no artist, of course, but I know a turkey when I see one. I've shot a hundred, and yours is the image of 'em. Why, sir, the autumn woods were all around me while I looked at it!"

"I thought I was alone in those woods," said Audubon. "It is pleasant, sir, to find you there."

Audubon was grateful to life for all small goodnesses; he did not fail to record this one. What he could not know, that day as he left the proud painter's door, was how fate would deal with Vanderlyn and with himself. For Audubon a deathless fame, a unique monument of achievement. For Vanderlyn, the death of the panorama's popularity, the Rotunda seized for debt, and the end which came to him alone and in the direst want. There is no adventure so high, or so full of hidden pitfalls, as art.

XVI

AS I go deeper into Audubon's life, and reach the richly documented phase of it, I have to carry an increasing number of reference books to and from the cabin in the woods. I came out this morning, through the blue-eyed balm of the spring day, burdened with them and with tobacco for many a long pipe, for I was going to see my saga through to the end now. I felt like Ronsard, who promised to lock himself into his room and read all Homer in one night. At the same time I had an impulse to throw the key of my cabin into the slough and lock myself out, to spend the day in the greening woods. Sunlight was gleaming on the umbrellas of the mandrake leaves; the high bright tops of the willows and cottonwoods above the slower trees threw up a salute. The flat-topped, layered hawthorns had the look of those thorn trees across the veldt, that I have never seen except in films of grazing giraffes. As outland, if you came to think of it, as a veldt tree was the tanager that flashed before me, just back from the Orinoco. The spring world has no walls. The young wind bears the thoughts away and away; the steel-blue, three-cornered shape of the swallow lifts the heart up with it; the unseen heron calls to the ears; the nostrils answer to the smell of the wild crab in flower; the curious simian hands ask for the twigs that snap off so neatly from the black willows around the sloughs. On the way to the cabin, it seemed, I had stepped on the wanderweed.

So I opened the door, chucked in everything I carried, and closed the door quickly before work should catch me. Past the big bur oaks I waded through the quaking, windy grass of a swale, hearing on my left the glee of the redwings whose note is like the ringing of doorbells to out-of-doors. Beyond the swale there is a long ridge covered with the climax forest of ash and basswood and oak, and I went there and found a sunny log to sit on and think.

Between two ash boles, down an aisle of shade, a great white trillium shone out like Venus in the evening sky. I feel about the trillium as a follower of Joan about the fleur-de-lys. There was one growing close to my foot, I saw, and I looked deeply at it, because there is a peculiar quality of depth to that flower. This lies, perhaps, in its plan of three, the Gothic trefoil exquisitely worked out, every stress balanced. The six-lobed ovary, the six long stamens, the three great pure petals arching equally out of the delicate three-fid calyx, and, supporting the whole design, the three great rhombic leaves. Down in the ground, the corm, a sphere that water and warmth had broken into this geometrical perfection in the air.

I had been looking at the trillium a long time before I realized that what I was thinking about was the way my hero's life had flowered perfectly from his single idea. Too few men grow from a single idea, and that a good one. It is an infallible design for a life.

I do not mean to say that Audubon was a perfect man. I may as well tell all his faults in one breath (for that is all they are worth). He was vain, personally and artistically, as the creative so often are—perhaps must be. His memory was untrustworthy and he was not too conscientious about it; he seldom spoiled a good story (when it was time for a story) for the truth. This he carried to such puckish lengths that he deceived a fellow naturalist, the half-mad genius Rafinesque, with tales of the "red-headed swallow" and the "diamond-scaled devilfish" of the Ohio, whose stony epidermis turns aside the bullet. Knowing Rafinesque's failing, Audubon knew that he would hasten to publish these creatures solemnly as new species, publish them to an American public which saw through tall tales, but received them with a straight face. Then Audubon went behind the barn, as it were, to have a good laugh. The world of science, with which the Audubon of the Henderson days was practically unacquainted, has however no sense of nonsense. The discredit for such fanciful species rebounded, of course, upon Audubon himself, since Rafinesque had ascribed them to his friend. So Audubon was charged, and still is, occasionally, with conscienceless nature faking, when in fact he was only perpetrating a frontier joke, such as Lincoln the lawyer might have got off on his friend Herndon of Springfield. Should you find a man in history who has no worse faults than these, you may well (if his virtues be as positive as Audubon's) go out for him with banners.

There are fashions in biography, the eulogistic fashion, the dry, impersonal, tedious fashion, the sprightly and superficial, and (to use some bastard but expressive English) the debunking fashion.

But I have never claimed that I am writing Audubon's biography; this is a salute to the man, perhaps even a salute to birds. As for an objective, impartial account of him, with dates, I have already contributed such a study to a dictionary of national biography. I have even written an article debunking him, in the debunker's monthly forum. Now I have come to praise him, not to bury him.

"This author"—I may as well write it for my critic—"has not hesitated to mix fact with fancy, and regards the subject of his memoir (for we can scarcely call it biography) as a national hero."

Quite so. This world has arrived at all its more spiritual levels because leaders, away out ahead of the rest of us, called to us and we followed. For all my disregard of it in these pages, I cannot even in these woods be unaware of the world beyond the woods, and the havoc in it. I know that while Audubon was looking at birds, the industrial revolution was beginning in New England, and that, aside from the pity he felt for its slaves, my hero did nothing about a question that, for many minds, filled all horizons and the sky. He turned his back in horror, and invited instead our attention to little blackburnian warblers, hovering on air as they flit in an ecstasy amongst blossoming hawthorns. While Manchester was a-building, out of women and children's bones, Keats listened to the nightingale. There are men who go into foul prisons, wash the leper, and take the stripes meant for others; there are those who lead us all out of the prison of self, the weary round of our getting and spending. Both, I say, are leaders of a religion, and it is religion by which we yearn to live. Some men will live by Buddha, some by Christ, some by Lenin, some by Gandhi.

I am one of the many to whom life itself is a religion. All life is in these woods, from seed to man, and its struggles and moralities are here, and not even under the surface. They stand out; they are what I am looking at. A hawk has just gone by with a screaming flicker in his talons; the hawk's mate waits-on, handsomely, to see where her lord will set down the banquet. What is the morality of the hawk and the flicker? Do not expect me to answer. I am only here to learn, and I shall die learning, like others always.

One man alone, in the wood, does not seem to represent adequately the struggle as it goes on outside. Nevertheless, I am part of it, and stand in judgment before those thousand creditors, my ancestors, my descendants, and my neighbors in life. I know no scales truer than those which balance what a man takes out of life against that which he gave it. Weighed in this way, John James Audubon balances as—if less than a leader—one who was nevertheless far in the vanguard.

Of what? Of that religion whose prophet we so need. No, certainly I cannot codify that religion in a set of commandments. I suspect that God gives commandments in plenty from on high, every day. I see better men than I am who must be living by them. Else how explain their courage in the face of all life's niggling and ignoble taxes, their tenderness with the helpless, their practiced creed that life is holy ground?

Life is holy ground. And thereon John James Audubon walked, with a woodsman's tread, venturing courageously on unbroken trails, missing not one bright wing in the bushes, exulting in the gift of life itself, passing it on as a creator to others.

I got up and went eagerly back to the cabin. No pleasure, after all, like talking about the thing you love.

Now I must shut my mind to my northern woods in their late swift spring, for Audubon is in Louisiana, first with the Pirrie family, and then, later when Lucy joined him with the children, in New Orleans. There were few crumbs, that winter, for the little family in Dauphine Street. Audubon had not even money to buy a blank-book for his journal. Perhaps, in any case, he thought it was better to keep no record of days so discouraging.

I seem to see him on a day that was cold, with a scud of icy rain in it, hurrying along Dauphine Street, his shoulders nearly to his ears, and his chest narrowed to the wind, his two sons trotting beside him. The boys did not know they were cold; their blood was nipping along to the tune of the story their father was telling them about the time he treed the cougar, and each one had one hand, at least, snug in a big fist and pocket. He would have them home before they knew it, and Lucy would be there to warm all three.

But Lucy wasn't home. The door closed behind them hollowly and the house was cold. Audubon stood looking around him, like a big tree with the leaves all gone, and the little boys waited, shivering out their feathers. She would be back, of course; but this moment had caught him unawares. It showed him with a shock how empty would stand his house of life without Lucy.

And, of course, she did come back, ten minutes later, and took off her bonnet and smoothed her hair.

"Well, John," she said, "I've found a position."

So, neatly, lightly and quietly, did Lucy always step into the breach. Wherever she went, women seem to have trusted Lucy. Her life long she found that other mothers were ready to give their children into her hands. She was to boast, in time, "If I can hold the mind of a young child to a subject for five minutes, he will never forget what I teach him." For this talent she was presently given scope at the Percy plantation in West Feliciana, where she held a little school for the Percy children and those of their aristocratic neighbors.

I wish that I could send my sons to that little school. Teaching today is a complicated marvel, directed—in all directions—by theoreticians of child psychology who have often very little feeling for children, and seem to me rather to play upon the child vice of sloth than the child's appetite to learn. I have a feeling that Lucy Audubon's theory of the way to teach was to teach. And when you really teach, that is to say, when some one learns from you, he learns you as well as the lesson.

That is why I wish I might send my sons to Lucy Audubon, with her inspired good sense.

After some months John was worked into the curriculum at the Percy plantation. He taught French, music, drawing and dancing to all the young folk of the countryside, and gave them lessons in swimming. It is a tradition in the Percy family that the ornithologist took his duties lightly, and spent most of his time in the woods. I am ready to assume this without any further corroboration. Many of his greatest drawings date from this period, and the text of his *Ornithological Biography* shows that the most intensive work of his life, in the field, was done in Louisiana. It became his habit to think of that state as the bird capital of the country. In describing the range and the prevalence of a species, he usually begins by telling whether or not it occurs in the state where the Mississippi finds the sea. The charm of Louisiana worked into his blood, and I can, myself, see how it might. There are pictures of it that have not faded for me after thirty years; they remain, far-off, but distinct and enticing as one of Audubon's own distant little backgrounds to a bird, such as the dreamy glimpse of a plantation all but obscured by the prominent grace of his *Snowy Heron.*

I remember the Mississippi, cutting through the middle of life, bronze and terrible, held up many feet above our heads between the long, snaky levees. I remember the crosses of unpainted wood all along the bank, which marked each the body of an unknown mouthful of the river. I remember the sugar cane, like wretched corn, standing in the half-flooded fields, and the glitter of the parish steeple in the incredible winter sunshine. There was the sweet, rotting smell of shallow waters warm in the sun, and the color of them which is such as sun may find in the heart of an old wine bottle. Black boys, who dragged up logwood from the river, black children with whom I must not play; black women who called through the lazy air from field to field, streaking it with golden echo. Their parrot laughter, flapping up over the screams of the guinea fowl. The black cook who came through the cypress swamp every day in her high snake boots, and talked an African French and made biscuits light as June clouds. The whites—so white in their faded gentility. A wind that went with a lonely sound saying, "Long ago, so long ago!" through the slim pines growing up in a

SNOWY HERON, OR WHITE EGRET

graveyard. Live oaks with generous arms and low-
bent, courteous heads. Camellias, outmoded, still
suiting Louisiana's mode.

Audubon has no adequate words for the happiness he had there: The mockingbirds sing all day
and all night... there are wrens chuck-a-luck-a-
lucking... yellowthroats whispering of witchery
... the thrashing of ivory-billed woodpeckers. He
can talk only in birds, as the birds themselves sing
wordlessly of their happiness.

The crown on his mood was the sense of achievement. The portfolios were bulging, he had found
his style and so far practiced it as to have pictures, he decided, enough for publication. He was
ready now in 1823 for the world. With his strip-
ling son Victor he journeyed for Kentucky, left
the boy with his aunt and uncle Berthoud, and
arrived in Philadelphia, the intellectual capital of
the country. His task was now to find a publisher
and subscribers for his work. He had to walk in
Wilson's footprints, and where that tragic little
Scot had gleaned the field with bleeding hands,
Audubon was now asking the public to accept and
pay for a work six times as costly.

And enemies lay in wait for him. They called
themselves Wilson's champions, but Wilson never

asked for the war that now ensued after his death. The hostility of Lawson, Wilson's engraver, was understandable; commerce supports rivalry. But in science the venom of a man like George Ord is forgivable but on one count—the lack of mental balance from which his warped soul suffered. "Not only cold water, but ice, was thrown upon all my undertakings," Audubon wrote to Lucy. But friends rallied to him. Thomas Sully gave him valuable lessons in the use of oils; Say, Mease, Harlan, and Charles Lucien Bonaparte, who had befriended Wilson and Rafinesque, did as well by the backwoodsman with the Frenchman's grace, though they could not secure his election to Philadelphia's most learned society. Edward Harris— who was to become the companion of Audubon's later expeditions—bought up from the long-haired stranger who found himself once more out of funds, every odd piece in the old portfolio, on sight and at the artist's own price.

Now I seem to have complained, a few pages back, that the artist, poor devil, is not kept on salary by the world. That may be true, but no one should know better than I that the sort of thing that Harris did for Audubon more frequently is done unto such poor devils than they deserve. There is an incomprehensible amount of generosity shown in this world to those who make it their business to create. I do not mean that they are overpaid—(Heaven forfend that I should betray my guild by such a suggestion). But some people who get no immediate good of the artist are often wondrous good to him.

Up to this point Audubon had received help and love from those who were close to him, but from now on he was destined to enjoy an extraordinary affection and assistance from strangers on two continents—Washington Irving, John Bachman, Daniel Webster, Edward Everett, Thomas Nuttall, to mention but a few in America, and, in Europe, open-hearted, wealthy patrons like the Rathbones of Liverpool, the naturalists of Edinburgh; but I am running out ahead of my tale. Here I would only claim for the recipient of all this aid and esteem that he had himself planted his happy destiny. It grew from a seed that he had buried deep in Kentucky's wild sod, in the dark years and the hard years. Now the tree was tall, the green deep tree full of flying birds. He had done a prodigious amount of hard and unique work, and now it was simply winning its first recognition.

Audubon saw Mill Grove again, but the phoebes' cave was gone; the rocks that had made it had been blasted away. Putting his mind on business (and for the first time it was business near his heart), he set out on his tour of the east in search of subscribers. That road was many years and thousands of miles long; it was chequered with disappointments and humiliations, but it was leading straight to success, a business success that the hard-heads who broke him might have envied.

Bonaparte, Napoleon's nephew, who enjoyed an equal fame as a bookish but genial naturalist on both sides of the Atlantic, urged Audubon strongly to take his drawings to Europe, where they could be properly engraved and better appreciated. This he seized upon as his goal. He was still flat in purse, as he traveled through the eastern cities, and still one of the unknown. And Lucy was still quietly teaching school at the Percy plantation.

It was one of those tender November mornings of the south; the plantation lay tranquil and indolent, breathing a shimmer of heat where the sun baked the fields. There was a stranger stagnation than usual on the land, for yellow fever was raiding the countryside; the town of West Feliciana had been deserted but for the postmaster and the doctor. The Percys had remained at home, and the children were continuing their lessons. In the schoolroom Lucy kept the morale at even temperature. Sums and round hand and the globe held sway over the young minds. Lucy's will quietly pervaded the room; the order of her dress implied a ruling order in this small universe; her level eyes looked out across the shining bent heads through the window towards the wall of the pine forest.

The Magna Charta, which was the subject of the next lesson, occupied the forefront of her mind, but its core thoughts were of John. She had been thinking of John for fourteen months, without a sight of him.

This I can say without hesitation. It is true, of course, that I must divine Lucy far more than her husband; she did not spread herself so artlessly on paper. I think of her as, more than all things, steady—this, partly from her recorded conduct, but more from the look of those extraordinarily level eyes that regard me both from the photographed bloom of youth and the wrinkled sockets of age. If I have failed to understand more of Lucy than her steadfastness, women, of all people, will perhaps forgive me. They keep their secrets;

they do not tell how much of their lives and spirits are poured into their men. I shall have to look at John to see Lucy.

And there, suddenly, in the schoolroom door he stands. He had slept in the woods that night; the rain had wet him and the brambles had torn him. He arrived, he says, "with rent and wasted clothes, and uncut hair, and altogether looking like the wandering Jew." Like Heaven to Lucy. The children were startled by a cry from their unshakable teacher. They saw her rush to the arms of the alarming tramp. Her clean sleeves went about his neck; her starched dress pressed to him; their lips were together. The boys, in embarrassment, curled up their toes inside their shoes and humped over their sums again. The girls looked from under their lashes, conscious that the secret of their lives was here, the root of life thrusting everywhere in dark plain earth, drinking for its need, the flower of life spread candid in its gleaming eclosion.

XVII

FROM New Orleans, Audubon set sail in the cotton schooner *Delos*, bound for Liverpool, with Lucy's savings of two years, and her blessings. In his pocket, jingling against her precious horde, was a little he had earned by teaching the country yokels of Mississippi to dance and fence. So, with his grace, and his rapier that was never drawn to kill, he had eked out that little more that was needed for his great cast. The gulls of America saw him out as far to sea as they dared. Then he was in mid-ocean, with the petrels' wings kissing water, or bearing them in one effortless, sideways tilt over the leaning mast.

The river voyage, between walls of the wilderness, is over. The sea, bordered by many lands, bears him away from me. A great wind is in the sails of his life. So my story must draw to its period. Finished are the wilderness years, the age of Audubon's passion and suffering and struggle, his archaic, his Homeric era. He passes now into the Golden Age of his conscious triumphs, his achievements before history. From this point forward, his life is intensely documented. You may read it for yourself, in his journals and letters and the memoirs of others about him. Future students, delving with a patience I do not own, will unearth details of the second half of Audubon's life span to add to the great mass already heaped up. For me there can be no further use. Drop the pilot, who knew only the invisible currents and shoals of the river.

I look through my open cabin door to the greening wall of the woods, empty but for the birds, and realize that only Lucy is left to me. Lucy, looking out across the bent heads of the schoolchildren, through the windows. Her eyes pass over the clearing where the bluejay sails with a long bragging whistle, and they stop at the dark circle of the forest, the wall of many doors. But he does not step out of any of them, with his dog and his gun and his smile.

Somewhere on the way there is a letter. She does not know if it is aboard a slow packet, lumbering in the trough of the waves, blowsing round Cape Sable like a sea-slattern, or staggering drunken up the Gulf in an off-shore wind. Is it rotting, that letter, in the old postoffice building in New Orleans? Is it squeezed in a sack flung over the back of an ambling nag picking her way from the river bayou? Will it lie on the shining mahogany console, in the hall of the house when she returns at evening? Or will there be only emptiness again, pity's kind smile with a shake of the head? Only emptiness in the great house where, a guest, a wife without a home, she carries her quiet dignity in her empty hands, walks, speaks, holds herself as a lady, and as a lady still, a lie in her eyes for their pity, goes up the sweep of the stairs to bed. But at night when the door is shut, and the lady's clothes slip down to the floor, she is only a woman, alone, with an aching loneliness, in the nights that stretch into weeks and lengthen unmercifully into the years.

But letters come; letters to crush against the breast, letters to read and re-read and to piece together, end to end, till they write her the book of her heart, the book of her life's dream.

First, Lucy read, John's pictures had been exhibited in Liverpool. The doors were jammed, and he cleared a hundred pounds. Next he was off to Scotland, armed with letters from noblemen, artists, and scientists. But what letter, John, will ever recommend you as you recommend yourself? Your smile, your eyes, your voice, your way with a man or a child or a dog—these speak for you, surely, these and your birds.

Lucy was ready, I think, or braced at least, for letters black with discouragement. She knew the volatility of her mate's temperament. And they came, of course. He had ever detested towns, and each new city, Liverpool, Manchester, Edinburgh, London and Paris, was like a tumble into icy water for him. The first word from Edinburgh showed Lucy how fast the mercury could fall, when she was not beside him. Professor Jameson, the eminent zoölogist, received Audubon with what the American fancied, at least, was coldness. The well-intrenched man seems to have told the uncertain newcomer, as the middle-class great are apt to do, that it was quite hopeless for Audubon even to attempt to peek into the top drawer. No, Sir Walter Scott would certainly not see him; he was writing a life of Napoleon and a new Waverley novel at the same time. And Sir Walter Scott, of course, was the lion rampant on Scotland's banner. You were not really accepted until he had noticed you. He, Jameson, would call to see those drawings—a little later, if he could find any time.

The very next letter showed the mercury up with a bound. An acquaintance had brought Lizars, the engraver of Selby's *British Birds*. Lizars had been silent a moment, shuffling over the great sheets. Then his eyes fell on the rattlesnake attacking the mockingbirds on their nest. "My God!" he cried, "I never saw anything like that before." He held up a few more, till he came to the great-footed hawks, with rags of bleeding flesh in their beaks, and their eyes gleaming with falcon lust. "Mr. Audubon," he promised, "the people here don't know who you are at all, but depend upon it, they *shall* know."

Lucy laughed aloud in her bedroom. Her secret, then, was out. It is only the years that have let out the secret of Lucy herself. The world, to paraphrase Lizars, had never heard of her then, but it *shall* know of her. Indeed, it does know of her that but for her vision and her effort John James Audubon might have grown old and simply silvered like a pine tree, indistinguishable from the rest of the backwoods. He might have finished out his days a loafer to the bone, a whittler of time, one of those American Raggedy Men so precious to the children of the up-and-coming.

Instead—"I am fêted, feasted, elected honorary

member of societies, making money by my exhibition and by my paintings. It is Mr. Audubon here,
and Mr. Audubon there, and I can only hope that
Mr. Audubon will not be made a conceited fool at
the last."

One night it was not a letter that lay on the
half-moon of mahogany in the stately hallway,
but a box. And when Lucy opened it, there tumbled out of the letter wrapped around it a golden
brooch, the sweetest trinket of Princes Street. I
think she loved it more for the pleasure he had
over it in that Edinburgh shop than for itself,
which was no more to her than many a parrot's
wing, or heron's bridal plume that he had brought
her when his pockets were empty.

The letter, smoothed out in her fingers, brought
its own golden freight. The crowds cannot even
get into the exhibition in the rooms of the Royal
Society. An expert has valued the painting of the
wild turkey cock at a hundred guineas. Yes, a
hundred golden guineas. Can you hear that, O
sharp and cautious men of Henderson, you little
wise men? You took all he had, and called it worthless. But you let something escape you, didn't you,
my friends? Something a little too bright for you
to see?

Then the presses actually flashed; the turkey cock, Plate I of *The Birds of America,* was pulled. The mighty Jameson descends from his perch. "Christopher North," the terrible arbiter of reputations in *Blackwood's Magazine,* has told the obedient world to admire. Lord Elgin, who carried the marbles out of the Parthenon frieze, stands up to drink a toast to Audubon. Sir Walter Scott sent for him and made him warmly welcome. Lucy heard all about the lion's white eyebrows, and quilted morning gown of light purple silk, and the round hand on the manuscript page, lying on the desk, of the next Waverley novel for which the world was waiting. She could not know what her John looked like to the delighted eyes of the old romancer:

"Mr. Audubon . . . is an American by naturalization, a Frenchman by birth, but less of a Frenchman than I have ever seen—no dash, or glimmer, or shine about him, but great simplicity of manners and behaviour; slight in person, and plainly dressed; wears long hair, which time has not yet tinged; his countenance acute, handsome and interesting, but still simplicity is the dominant characteristic."

Nothing is harder for an American to achieve

than personal popularity in Europe. In Britain particularly he is not viewed simply as a foreigner, but as an embarrassing relative. But when a trans-Atlantic really carries the Old World before him, he generally succeeds by virtue of an intense Americanism, like Franklin's or Lindbergh's, or Audubon's.

This came out clearly when Audubon went on to London. Hackles at first rose along many a spine, whether London saw him as an American backwoodsman, or a Frenchman, or an artist, or a scientist who was breaking with tradition in scientific illustration, and that with a happy freedom that was flagrant. The world was ready to agree with Lizars that they had never seen anything like that before! Loud protests were sometimes raised, some from museum men who had said that the attitudes were anatomically impossible, some from naturalists of the gray-eyed island where Nature is a silvery, delicate, and subtle affair, who protested that such plumage and such flowers might be a new phase of the well-known American exaggeration. There was even one, an excellent scientist, who set out to illustrate his ornithology of India, guided chiefly, it is said, by the discreet desire to "avoid the exaggerations of

Audubon." The result was recognized at once as something insipid, outdated, pre-Audubon. What a fool's fate, to fail through having tried so hard not to be like a great man!

For, when the protesting throats were hoarse and finally mute, the fact remains that the Audubon style spoiled the public for anything less lifelike. It had an effect comparable to the introduction of perspective into painting. The great bird painters of today may surpass Audubon, in sheerly technical ways, for it is easy for a later century to improve on the technique invented in an earlier one. But Rex Brasher and Frank Benson and all others employ the Audubon touch. It is simply the living touch.

One of the unforeseen results of the wave of enthusiasm on which Audubon was finally borne aloft was a revival of interest in Wilson's *American Ornithology*. Before Audubon was ready, a corps of British workers were hastening a second edition of the little weaver's book into print. One of those buccaneers of publishing rushed out with an Audubonized Wilson—the drawings of the Scot given life in the new manner. He failed, of course; and the legitimate undertaking of a second edition of

Wilson only served to sell itself and Audubon together to the public.

American Nature has always been capable of arousing an astonishing enthusiasm in the Old World, even among those who have never seen it and cannot hope to. And that latent emotion welled up and bore Audubon along to triumph. No other discoverer from Europe's shores, not the conquistadores, laden with gold, nor Raleigh with his redskins led to kneel at Elizabeth's throne, brought back so truly the New World they had found.

Rather naturally, it was a Frenchman, a well known critic of the time, who put down with most generous sympathy his impression of the Royal Society exhibition. "We have admired in the rooms of the Royal Society of Edinburgh," wrote Philarète-Chasles, "the public exhibition of [Audubon's] original water-color drawings. A magic power transported us into the forests which for so many years this man of genius has trod. Learned and ignorant alike were astonished at the spectacle which we will not attempt to reproduce.

"Imagine a landscape wholly American, trees, flowers, grass, even the tints of the sky and the waters, quickened with a life that is real, peculiar, trans-Atlantic. On twigs, branches, bits of shore, copied by the brush with the strictest fidelity, sport the feathered races of the New World, in the size of life, each in its particular attitude, its individuality and peculiarities. Their plumages sparkle with nature's own tints; you see them in motion or at rest, in their plays and their combats, in their anger fits and their caresses, singing, running, asleep, just awakened, beating the air, skimming the waves, or rending one another in their battles. It is a real and palpable vision of the New World, with its atmosphere, its imposing vegetation, and its tribes which know not the yoke of man. The sun shines athwart the clearing in the woods; the swan floats suspended between a cloudless sky and a glittering wave; strange and majestic figures keep pace with the sun, which gleams from the mica sown broadcast on the shores of the Atlantic; and this realization of an entire hemisphere, this picture of a nature so lusty and strong, is due to the brush of a single man; such an unheard of triumph of patience and genius!— the resultant rather of a thousand triumphs won in the face of innumerable obstacles!"

Subscribers flocked to Audubon's list; their first installments were paid in; they awaited their plates, when suddenly Lizars threw up the job.

The Birds of America might have died still-born
had not Audubon walked on a lucky morning into
the engraving shop of the Havells, father and son.
The son, a gifted draughtsman, was given a drawing for reproduction as a test. A few days later,
Audubon came back to see the results. He held up
the sheet, inspecting every line on every pinion,
and laid it down with a great swelling in his chest.
Then to the astonishment and horror of the young
Englishman, the artist threw his arms about his
neck and whirled him in a rigadoon around the
room, shouting—with a most inaccurate feeling
for English argot—"Ze jig is up! Ze jig is up!"
The Havells made Audubon's fortune, but it is no
less true that he made theirs. With an immense
reputation derived from *The Birds of America*,
they built up a business that enabled them both
to retire at an early age.

With Queen Adelaide's subscription in his
pocket, Audubon set off for the conquest of Paris.
As fame on the banks of the Forth counts for
nothing beside the Thames, so English approval
feels cold by the Seine. Yet the capture of Paris
was easy. The mighty Cuvier, incredibly powerful, terrifyingly ugly, stamped Audubon's science
with his fiat. The Duke of Orleans told restored

PLATE. CCIX

Forked-tailed Petrel.
THALASSIDROMA LEACHII.
Male & Female.

FORK-TAILED PETREL

Drawn From Nature by J.J.Audubon. F.R.S.F.L.S.

Engraved Printed & Coloured by R. Havell. London, 1831.

Bourbons to think highly of his art. And Charles
Lucien Bonaparte was at hand to marshal the
Bonapartistes.

What America will grovel before is a son that
it has rejected who has carried European capitals.
The return of Audubon to "America, my country,"
as his motto ran, partook of the sort of triumph
that is known to the diva from Medicine Hat and
La Scala. Newspapers reported all his movements;
they featured his explorations, to Labrador, to
Florida, to Texas, to Wyoming. Presidents Jackson and Houston were proud to shake his hand, sir.
Precious collections were unlocked for him, a yacht
offered him for bird-nesting up the waterways.

The rest of his active life was spent in the field,
or in Europe superintending publication of the
Birds, the *Ornithological Biography*, and *The
Quadrupeds of America*. The *Ornithological Biography* was an afterthought intended to accompany
the bird drawings; its value, aside from the scientific descriptions which were put in by William
MacGillivray, and its charm lie in the personal
narratives—Audubon's recollections of that first
moment when his feathered subject flew across his
sight. He is not the graceful writer that Thomas
Nuttall is, but even though his English is some-

times stilted I still like it better than Wilson's earnest pedestrian style. The *Quadrupeds* contain many of Audubon's experiences with the four-footed, and the paintings are in the Audubon style, but most of them are the work of his sons and most of the text—very excellent text—can be ascribed to the Reverend John Bachman of Charleston.

The last years of the great life passed in tranquillity, his wife, his sons and their wives around him in the Audubon home above the Hudson. Here he dwelt, the Hudson River sage, the patriarch, the half-saint about whom legend already clustered—legend that, I fancy, he did little to destroy. And it is to this phase of his life, and only to this, that a scrupulous biographer might ascribe the virtue of enthusiasm for wild life conservation. The destruction of trusting sea fowl by the eggers of Labrador seems to have wakened in Audubon this passion which he now symbolizes.

It is savory to know that there in his home on the Hudson the grand old man received, with warm cordiality, his old partner and opposite, Ferdinand Rozier. Rozier himself was now a patriarch, father of ten, master of means, as big a man in Ste. Geneviève, Missouri, as Audubon in London or Paris. And in further conviviality, both old gentlemen were the honored guests, in New York, of the stout-hearted and sympathetic Nicholas Berthoud.

Long before the spirit took wing from the weathered body, a twilight fell upon John James Audubon. So much had he seen and felt, so widely lived, so greatly loved, beyond the limits of common men, that now the exerted forces failed. The mind dimmed. In that gentle dusk he knew that his Lucy was there, and his strong sons. He was aware, at times, that men came bringing him yet more honors, but he no longer felt them.

The twilight deepened. In the shadows were shapes, people who pitied him, people he loved and was forgetting. When he walked beneath the trees an arm was slipped under his arm, supporting him; hands dressed him gently. And then he was dressed no longer.

Strangers were around his bed, strange faces that suddenly cleared and were those of his children and his wife. The shadows veiled him; the strangers were there again, and then there were voices, requiring of him a few last simple acts of living.

The tired lids fell, and it seemed that his sight cleared. He could see Lucy, bright and young, Lucy in the schoolroom, looking up and finding him, flying to his arms. Lucy with a finger on her grave lips—was the child asleep? Lucy weeping, for whose death he did not know. For the little dead daughters in cold Kentucky sod?

Who was it who lay dead or dying? His mother, Anne, Anne Moynet Audubon? *"Est-ce toi, ma mère, qui m'a tant aimé? Est-ce toi, maman?"*

A hand covered his, kind as a mother's, kind as a wife's. For a great darkness was coming up over the sky, and there was the rushing of a kingdom of wings. It was the pigeons, he thought one moment clearly, the passenger pigeons that stretched like a dark rainbow over the wilderness. For a moment he knew the black glory of the flight sweeping over him.

So passed death's wings. It was a little moment, that of dying, and after came a long immortality. The life that he lived has not gone out of the world. What he loved is here, the trillium, the tanager's wing, the broken half of a bluebird's egg tumbled on the young grass under the oaks. What he wrought out of what he loved remains, living and imperishable.

I look up to my walls, to the barn swallows home-keeping under the old beam, to the petrels lost at sea and the winter wren in his little world of moss and toadstool, and I fling up my hand to them, old friend, in high salute.

SOURCES

For a nearly complete bibliography of books and papers by and about Audubon, the reader should see that contained in *Audubon the Naturalist*, by Francis Hobart Herrick (full citation below). Here it is intended merely to mention the actual sources from which the historical skeleton of this book is constructed, without attempting to include many other narratives of his life, various letters to or from Audubon, which have been reprinted from time to time, speeches, reminiscences and other miscellaneous documentation, most of which has been collated and digested by Herrick.

Principal Biographical and Autobiographical Writings

Audubon, John James: *Ornithological Biography*. 5 vols. Edinburgh, 1831-1839. There is also an American reprint of this work, which is intended as a text to accompany *The Birds of America*. Besides the many incidents in his life as an ornithologist which Audubon here mentions in direct connection with particular species, there are interspersed through the first four volumes a miscellany of brief episodes in his life, either with animals or fellow humans, or sheer descriptions of the American scene, which Audubon called "Episodes of Western Life." These have ever formed a rich mine for the biographer, and some authors, like Buchanan and Burroughs, have pieced out, with extracts from such of his journals as were then available, a whole biography. Graphic and interesting as are these "Episodes" and, in many cases, doubtless true to fact, others are strongly tinged by Audubon's desire to make a smooth running story, so that he commingles, as if they were coincident, events that are proven to have happened at widely different times.

Audubon, Maria R.: "Audubon's Story of his Youth." *Scribner's Magazine*, vol. xiii, pp. 267-287. New York, 1893. This was the first appearance of autobiographical material entitled "Myself," J. J. Audubon.

Buchanan, Robert (editor) : *The Life and Adventures of John James Audubon, the Naturalist*. Edited from materials supplied by his widow. London, 1868. This work had a second and third English edition and is now available in "Everyman's Library." Buchanan had before him a wealth of first-hand material rich in American life, letters, and lore, for which the gifted English poet, who regarded this as a hackwork job, had no feeling. He boiled it down, as he says, to one fifth of its prolix condition, smoothed out Audubon's style into something more acceptable to the British public of the day, and added a few rather hostile remarks upon Audubon himself, assuming at all times a condescending attitude toward the naturalist. In spite of all these faults, Buchanan's work does constitute one of the first extended accounts of Audubon's life to which any importance attaches, for it is compiled from the "Episodes" mentioned above and the journals of the naturalist.

Audubon, Lucy (editor): *The Life of John James Audubon, the Naturalist.* Edited by his Widow. With an Introduction by James Grant Wilson. New York, 1869. This differs but little from Buchanan's biography, mentioned above, except that whatever of hostility or condescension marked the Englishman's biography has been expunged. It has often been reprinted.

Audubon, Maria R.: *Audubon and His Journals. With zoölogical notes by Elliott Coues.* 2 vols. New York, 1898. Until the appearance of the Herrick boigraphy this was by far the most complete and valuable of accounts. Its faults are a tendency to smooth out all asperities in the life and character of Audubon and his family and friends, and to continue old quarrels and make numerous charges against Audubon's real or fancied enemies, which might better have been left to die, either because they are unfounded or not worth remembering. Miss Audubon, the naturalist's granddaughter, either did not know the true story of Audubon's parentage, or she suppressed it, and she perpetuates many other mistakes of less importance as to place, date and deed. It remains, however, a source of immense importance and interest. I am indebted to Charles Scribner's Sons for permission to quote certain passages from this work.

Herrick, Francis Hobart: *Audubon the Naturalist. A History of His Life and Time.* 2 vols. New York, 1917. To this work every modern student owes an immense debt for its painstaking methods, correcting as it does great masses of error in all earlier accounts. Above all, the author must be thanked for his unearthing of the true story of the naturalist's birthplace, birth date, and parentage, for his account of the life of Audubon's father in Haiti and Nantes, and his studies of the ornithologist's little-known childhood and young manhood in France, Pennsylvania, and Kentucky. I am grateful to this author and to D. Appleton and Co., his publishers, for permission to quote from this excellent work. It is especially valuable for its chronology of Audubon's life, its bibliography of books and papers by and about him, and its fine illustrations.

Corning, Howard (editor): *Journal of John James Audubon, made during his trip to New Orleans in 1820-21.* Foreword by Ruthven Deane. Boston, 1929. This is an entirely unchanged journal covering the last portion of my book, except for the final chapter, which has seen publication since the

Herrick biography. It is fascinating reading because in no way polished, expurgated, smoothed out or abbreviated. I acknowledge gratefully permission from The Club of Odd Volumes to quote from this journal.